G. C. Fair

Rolla, Mo.

May 18, 1954

'A RIGHT JUDGMENT IN ALL THINGS'

'A RIGHT JUDGMENT IN ALL THINGS'

Austin Pardue

FOREWORD BY LAURISTON L. SCAIFE

GREENWICH · CONNECTICUT · 1954

TO ALL THOSE WHO ARE TRYING TO PLAY

CRICKET WITH THE SPIRIT OF THE GOSPEL

I am glad to have the privilege of commending Austin Pardue's *A Right Judgment in All Things*. It is one of those volumes which speaks to the heart and mind of "all sorts and conditions of men." From these pages pours a steady flow of hope. It inspires to new heights the spiritually and ethically strong; encourages the weak, suffering, and despondent; and gives new vision to the fallen and neglected.

Though the central theme of this book is not prayer, in the presentation of life's problems and opportunities, the place and power of prayer are vividly portrayed. The ability of prayer to influence right decisions, give new horizons to the sick and handicapped, and weld bonds of creative and eternal relationship with Almighty God, is vividly illustrated and proclaimed from the author's own experience.

To a degree the book is autobiographical for the author openly considers the pitfalls in his own life. He does not hesitate to reveal dangerous and weak areas of his own experiences as he has faced trials, temptations, and opportunities. It is refreshing to have a man of spiritual stature disclose the ramifications of his life in such a way that most of us are able to profit by his experience. He forthrightly meets practical issues of day by day conduct at home and at work which require the application of Christian ethics.

Too often the Christian way of life is conceived of as being impossible to realize in our modern world, but Bishop Pardue forcefully illustrates the practicability and advantages of such living. The certainty of the Christian ethic as practiced for everyday living grows increasingly certain as fact, illustration, and reason multiply in each succeeding chapter.

Many points are driven home, explained, and proved by reference to appropriate quotations from the Holy Bible and the Book of Common Prayer. Modern application of truth gleaned from these ancient yet eternal Books fortifies the ethic under discussion and inspires the reader with renewed certainty and inspiration.

Herein the reader may find a blueprint for peace of mind and soul. The way to spiritual and mental health is categorically pointed out to those who are willing to accept the prescription. The author describes the growing development of small groups within the established framework of the Church. Many of their participants have become living examples of the power of the Holy Ghost to influence their lives toward better health, serenity, and Christian action.

The theology of the book is sound and is written in the language of the day, thereby making it easily understood. The depth of wisdom contained therein or the value of precepts proclaimed do not suffer because of the book's readability. It makes a strong appeal to one's better nature and re-emphasizes the indestructible link between theology and practical living.

LAURISTON L. SCAIFE

CONTENTS

xi

CONTENTS

CONTENTS

PROLOGUE

PROLOGUE

What more does a man need today than a right judgment in every decision and action he undertakes, together with the spiritual courage to stand by the judgment if it is right and once it is made? Let us learn from Jesus.

Matthew 14:13-24
When Jesus heard of it, he departed thence by ship into a desert place apart: and when the people had heard thereof, they followed him on foot out of the cities. And Jesus went forth, and saw a great multitude, and was moved with compassion toward them, and he healed their sick. And when it was evening, his disciples came to him, saying, This is a desert place, and the time is now past; send the multitude away, that they may go into the villages, and buy themselves victuals. But Jesus said unto them, They need

3

not depart; give ye them to eat. And they say unto him, We have here but five loaves, and two fishes. He said, Bring them hither to me. And he commanded the multitude to sit down on the grass, and took the five loaves, and the two fishes, and looking up to heaven, he blessed, and brake, and gave the loaves to his disciples and the disciples to the multitude. And they did all eat and were filled: and they took up of the fragments that remained twelve baskets full. And they that had eaten were about five thousand men, beside women and children. And straightway Jesus constrained his disciples to get into a ship, and to go before him unto the other side, while he sent the multitudes away. And when he had sent the multitudes away, he went up into a mountain apart to pray: and when the evening was come, he was there alone. But the ship was now in the midst of the sea, tossed with waves: for the wind was contrary.

The episode of the Feeding of the Five Thousand was one of the great turning points of history. Our Lord faced a momentous decision which called for a right judgment. The situation that developed as a result of the meal was one that called for a clear, objective insight and the courage to follow it through with action. This was accomplished. Its effects will be felt throughout eternity. What is more, it has a very personal application for you and me today.

4

We are not asked to fathom the full import of the event, but we are asked to glean enough significance from it to help us discover some of the secrets of His poise and calm and to learn how to use these secrets in the midst of the many crises which dog the footsteps of each one of us daily.

Jesus knew only too well that the frothy experience of being with too many people too much of the time was exhausting and drained one of the energy and the ability to see with clarity. Just prior to the episode we are considering, He went by ship across the Sea of Galilee to a lonely desert place. He wanted to get away from the crowd, but the multitude followed Him.

He had a mysterious quality about Him then, as He has now, that magnetized all those who saw Him. When He arrived at the other side of the Sea of Galilee, many were already awaiting His debarkation from the small boat in which He had been traveling, while others were wearily trudging around the lake, over the rough terrain, to meet Him when He landed. Within a short time, therefore, He found Himself again preaching to the people and healing their sick.

Toward evening, His disciples became concerned for the physical welfare of His devotees. It was sug-

5

gested that He send them away to the various towns where they could get the food they all so badly needed by that time.

These were the circumstances, and it is clear that Our Lord had taken no anxious thought for the multitude and had not planned a meal in terms of a miracle. The supernatural was as natural to Him as breathing. It merely meant that He called upon His knowledge of the laws of God which men of the earth do not as yet understand. (Just as a hundred years ago, we did not understand the laws of aerodynamics and we now can fly—yet, the secrets of aerodynamics have existed from the beginning of time.) So, He told His leaders not to send the crowd home. Instead, He simply ordered that they be fed. But how? The disciples said that they had only five loaves and two small fishes. Jesus responded by asking that such food as was there be brought to Him.

When this was done, Jesus turned to the enthralled multitude and told them to sit down on the ground. He began to celebrate a prelude to the mystery of the Holy Communion and lost Himself in prayer. Power and grace came upon the elements of food in front of Him. Somehow, He transmuted His energy into mate-

6

rial form and multiplied the food in front of Him so that there was sufficient to feed everyone present. He lowered the eyes that had been lifted in prayer. The bread that had been blessed, He broke. Then He called upon His disciples for an orderly distribution of the meal. He was exposing them and the people to more than physical sustenance. He was offering them a portion of the spiritual power that lies back of the operation of the universe. They were not ready to receive it.

After the meal, according to custom, He ordered His followers to gather up the fragments that remained over and above the needs of the people. In those times the practice of such food gathering after a feast was carefully observed, especially after a spiritual feast, for men were called upon to beware lest they presume upon the Divine bounty. It was common belief that when food was not preserved after a meal, demons would possess the wasteful people. People can so easily forget God when they have more than enough of this world's bounty. The responsibility of good stewardship is always to be pressed upon Christians, for wastefulness and self-indulgence are sins of serious proportions. The devil always inhabits wastefulness.

Before they were through eating, Jesus realized

7

that to the multitude present the feast was a fabulous success. The people were ecstatic over the miracle; their viewpoint was mundane. They had missed the spiritual quality to which they had been exposed. They thought only in terms of the materialistic use to which this Man of Power could be put. Before their eyes, they believed, stood a man with such dynamic leadership and miraculous capacities that He could lead their downtrodden race of humiliated Jews back to Jerusalem, decapitate Herod, and Himself take the throne. Roman rule would be put down, and they would be exalted.

Jesus was not in the least fooled. He recognized their hate-filled and revengeful gloating over an anticipated military success. Consequently, from our Lord's viewpoint, the spiritual feast was a dismal failure, and this experience drew a climactic line across His ministry. He saw clearly that miracles for the multitude lead only to mass hysteria and a superficial following.

Suppose the Roman government had been overthrown and the chosen race had again been restored to power. He realized that it would make little difference, for a change in government did not mean a change of heart. Fundamentally, the hearts of the Jews were no closer to the Kingdom of God than the hearts of the

8

Romans. The religion of both had degenerated into a great yearning for power and gain. There was no point in substituting one selfish government for another. His objective was to dethrone pride or selfishness from its dominant place in the human heart. He realized that now He must withdraw to pray and think through His plans for the future. How was He truly to redeem men? He began to see that His popularity must be sacrificed for the truth which alone could set men free from the enslavement of their human weaknesses. He called His leaders together and told them to go to the boat and immediately embark for the other shore, saying that He would dismiss the crowd and send them home.

Peter was probably as disappointed as anyone. Was he not the chief of the disciples and had he probably not entertained high hopes of being appointed prime minister, secretary of state, or minister of war? He tried to protest, but with a quick glance and a short word, he was silenced.

The disciples climbed into the ship and silently shoved off into the blackness of an approaching storm. Jesus turned to the stunned multitude and in a few words sent them back to their dwelling places.

It was evening, and in the fading light His heart

9

was heavy and compassionate. His body was weary. He raised His eyes to the mountain ahead. Strength returned. Silently and alone He started to climb the steep ascent with certain strides and a strengthening song, "I will lift up mine eyes unto the hills . . . My help cometh even from the Lord" (Ps. 121:1). There He would meet His Father face to face and would map a course for the future. By the time darkness had fallen, He had found His favorite spot, and soon He was enveloped in the flaming silence of the All-knowing, All-loving, All-powerful Presence.

AN ANCIENT GUIDE

CHAPTER ONE

AN ANCIENT GUIDE

The objective of this book is to study a few of the universal principles of Jesus in order to minimize the paralyzing effects of confusion, indecision, and anxiety upon human beings. There are definite ways and means by which we can reach right decisions. Then, having made them, there are further means by which we may receive the strength to stand by them and act upon them until such time as they be accomplished.

By virtue of the immutability of spiritual law, a person who is "right" will finally win every confusing encounter. It is possible to experience Paul's counsel

13

when he said, "Having done all, stand," and to experience this with the apostle's sane, calm confidence. Furthermore, it is possible to attain this state of consciousness, and to maintain it most of the time, if we follow the gospel principles of our Lord.

We approach this book from our personal experience in seeking to solve our problems, past, present, and future. Through diligent search, we have found, what is for us, a helpful formula, indeed a life-changing process. This book is primarily a testimony. It arose out of personal frustrations that were alleviated and very often solved by a search of the Scriptures, by continued prayer, by conversations with wise spiritual teachers, and by practical revelations of the truth of God. These suggestions have worked for us and have, moreover, helped in the process of changing the lives of others. We offer them as guideposts "along the way," a way which we now traverse. A road that is long, and a road that stretches far ahead.

We do not approach this subject from the point of view of the logician who proceeds along the lines of pure reason. We approach the theme from the point of view of the spiritual and mystical. We encourage the study of logic, but such books should be written by specialists in that field. The basis of our viewpoint is to be found in the ancient Collect or prayer for Whitsunday.[1]

If you desire to have a right judgment in all things and want the strength to follow the same with action, this Collect of the ancient Christian Church awaits your praying. That is the first sure and certain step toward victory. This is the "ancient guide":

O God, who as at this time didst teach the hearts of thy faithful people, by sending to them the light of thy Holy Spirit; Grant us by the same Spirit to have a right judgment in all things, and evermore to rejoice in his holy comfort; through the merits of Christ Jesus our Saviour, who liveth and reigneth with thee, in the unity of the same Spirit, one God, world without end. *Amen.* (*P.B.*, p. 180.)

This prayer or Collect for Whitsunday is derived from what is known as the "Gregorian Sacramentary" —an ancient collection of prayers. "The noteworthy point in this Collect," says Dr. Massey H. Shepherd, Jr., "is its teaching that we may rejoice in the comfort (i.e.

---

[1] The other name for Whitsunday is Pentecost which means the fiftieth day after Easter (taken over by the Church from Judaism). The English and other northern European peoples called this day "White Sunday," from the white garments worn by the newly baptized.

strength) of the Holy Spirit only if we allow Him to guide our judgment 'in all things.' The Spirit first illumines our minds with the discernment of true and righteous courses of action, and then He strengthens our wills so that we may accomplish His will with joy."[2]

The ancient prayer is packed with powerful energy for those who will learn it by heart and say it consciously when waking and subconsciously when sleeping. It has been said in the past by millions of people, millions of times, at thousands of altars the world over, through centuries of human experience. It has been tried and proved not wanting. Today, we tend to say it as so many parrots, and, through repetition without thought (a method that destroys serious belief), it has become smooth and worn. It stands, however, in the Book of Common Prayer ready to be prayed. Its potential effects are awaiting the magnetic force of a faith that will, in turn, set God's power free to perform effective action and win satisfying results.

A second important step toward the attainment of the inward peace that comes from the knowledge of

---

[2] Massey H. Shepherd, Jr., *The Oxford American Prayer Book Commentary* (New York: Oxford, 1950), p. 180. Used by permission of the publisher.

16

right judgment is the practice of openness to the truth at all times as it relates to ourselves, our families, our friends, our enemies, and our possessions. We must so love the truth that we can rejoice when we discover that we are on the wrong track. When we are wrong, we must admit it with gratitude and alacrity. Thus, it is possible to get back on the right track no matter how wrong we have been or how confused our paths. When we know the fundamental principles and are willing to follow them, we will delight in the fact that He always "giveth us the victory."

Each one of us, no matter who we are, has one common tendency and that is to evade, distort, and deny unpleasant facts about ourselves or those persons and institutions to whom we give affection and allegiance. This is the way it has been all through history. Not only do we make excuses, but we generally project blame on innocent people and events. The Greeks blamed the gods for their ailments. The Hindus and Buddhists place responsibility for evil experiences upon their Karma or difficulties due to past lives lived in other bodies which now cannot be remembered. The Mohammedans blame Kismet. People of all races and colors have excused their mistakes by

17

blaming the stars, the moon, or some other mysterious hand of fate. The twentieth century intellectual tends to blame his environment, his glands, or the promptings of his subconscious mind. The Republicans blame the Democrats, the Democrats blame the Communists, and the Communists blame the Capitalists (Republicans). Granted that all of these factors may have certain negative influences upon our lives, granted that all of them may help create difficulties for us, nevertheless, there is no situation that cannot be overcome by victory through prayer and faith in God.

Study yourself and your friends as objectively as is humanly possible and note how they have cleverly, and usually without conscious knowledge, been able to concoct blame for misfortune by making other people or situations responsible. In many instances, the individual himself is blind to his own mistakes. It is the uncommon thing to find a person who is objective and so able to face his own life with humility that he can admit it if his attitudes are wrong. Humility is one of the rarest of all qualities, and as a great American industrialist said recently: "True humility is the one great ingredient for success in any field, for without it a man ceases to be teachable."

18

Let us note in passing that we do not want to send people into a state of despair over their past mistakes. Christianity tells you to admit them, and then teaches that you can be forgiven in Christ's name. Neither do we want anyone to become morbidly introspective about his actions. We seek to fulfill the spirit of the Gospel which tells us to be as tolerant and loving of ourselves as we are of others. We are admonished to "love our neighbors as ourselves." It is a virtue to love yourself if, of course, you love your neighbor to the same extent. Then you cannot go far wrong, and neither can you lash yourself with the hideous thongs of masochistic imaginings. If we seek to understand ourselves, our minds and muscles will be released from tension, and we will begin to know the peace about which so few have any understanding.

As we have said, logic and reason are indispensable to human needs, but you do not need to be a Thomas Aquinas to obtain a right judgment or action. The average Christian need only believe that "the faith once delivered to the Saints" as revealed through the Bible and the Church is sufficient for the average wayfarer's needs.

Is it not true that all the individual and collective

19

tragedies of the world, past or present, are, have been, and will be, the consequence of judgment based on self-centered human faculties that have not sought the wisdom of the Holy Spirit? We may here listen to the words of St. Augustine:

For it is not by having flesh, which the Devil has not, but by living according to himself—that is, according to man—that man became like the Devil. For the Devil, too, wished to live according to himself when he did not abide in the truth; so that when he lied, it was not of God but of himself, who is not only a liar but the father of lies, he being the first who lied, and the originator of lying as a sin.

When, therefore, man lives according to man, and not according to God, he is like the Devil because not even an Angel might live according to an Angel, but only according to God, if he was to abide in the truth, and speak God's truth and not his own lie. When, then, a man lives according to the truth, he lives not according to himself, but according to God; for He was God who said, 'I am the truth.' When, therefore, man lives according to himself—that is, according to man, not according to God—assuredly he lives according to a lie; not that man himself is a lie, for God is his author and creator, who is certainly not the author and creator of a lie, but because man was made upright, that he might not live according to himself, but according to him that made him—in other words, that he might do his will

20

and not his own; and not to live as he was made to live, that is a lie.[3]

When egocentric, and therefore self-interested judgments are the basis of action, evil results must follow. Grapes do not come from thistles. The science of living rests upon the same premises as do the physical and natural sciences of the universe: cause and effect. Consequently, if you have "the right judgment" and follow it up with the right action, you must, by the nature of spiritual law, obtain the right results.

This book, as has been said, is written out of past sufferings which came from mistaken actions based on bad judgment and selfish whims. These we seek to correct by the grace of God through the wisdom of inner illumination from the Holy Spirit—plus common sense. Here, we are attempting from our own experience to live a life more familiar with victory and less harassed by defeat.

No matter how tense, tired, and defeated one may be, the victory through Christ can be had. Whether this book will help gain this experience can only be proved by an attempt to practice that which we suggest. We hasten to add that we continue to have our

---

[3] Augustine, *Confessions* XIV, § 3-4.

own frustrations and problems, but our hope of victory is tenfold compared to the confusion of past times. What we outline in this book has helped us immeasurably. And what we speak of here, we actually know as fact; namely, that the fundamental laws of God work with the precision and accuracy of the laws of nature or physics or chemistry (which of course are part of the laws of God).

WE MUST BE RIGHT—UNDER GOD

CHAPTER TWO

WE MUST BE RIGHT—UNDER GOD

It is a man's duty as a Christian to study to be right. It is far more than a duty, however, it is the essence of his own security, future happiness, and ultimate success in the experience of living. When you are right, failure is an impossibility even though all the surrounding circumstances conspire against you. Evil antagonism is a mere mirage of the Devil's own making in the hope that you will succumb to the judgment of men and receive the reward of disintegrating destruction.

A conviction of being right that is grounded in the Word of God is a strong Christian virtue for people to possess in the midst of human pressures, dissensions, and bitter resentments. Imagine what it means to possess the peace of God! Then only can you stand alone with Him against the multitude because you are convinced that, together, your righteousness will assuredly prevail.

Alan Richardson, in his *A Theological Word Book of the Bible,* discusses the meaning of being right or possessing righteousness.[1] He shows that throughout the ages the concept is ever growing and that it has more than a mere ethical connotation. It implies firmness and resolution toward right action and fair dealing between man and man. Furthermore, it has a strong emphasis within its orbit that relates to certain victory by virtue of the fact that righteousness is in union with God's final and universal law. God's law must ultimately triumph and so must he who is aligned with it. In the New Testament it is linked inseparably with the emphasis upon salvation. Salvation means the ultimate preservation and saving of a soul, because that soul undeservedly has been embraced by the unlimited and all protecting power of God Himself. St. Paul uses the phrase "belief

---

[1] Alan Richardson *A Theological Word Book of the Bible* (New York: Macmillan, 1951), p. 202 ff.

unto righteousness" as almost synonymous with "faith unto salvation."

What are the steps that you and I may take toward the attainment of this cherished state of spiritual, physical, mental, and emotional health? Are they any other than renouncing our sinful pride and thus depending on God and seeking His grace? We must depend on God because we alone cannot save ourselves from ourselves and without the grace of God "there is no health [strength] in us." The only redemptive power we have is God's gift, and this is not self-generated. Let us look deeper into the saving power that comes to every Christian from faith.

Prayers in the Book of Common Prayer abound in a quality of utter dependence upon God. With a confident approach to "a right judgment," one experiences this assurance of Divine security. Such phrases as these are continually appearing:

O Lord, raise up, we pray Thee, Thy power and come among us, and with great might succor us . . . speedily help and deliver us.

Grant . . . that in all our sufferings here upon earth for the testimony of thy truth, we may stedfastly look up to Heaven, and by faith behold the glory that shall be

27

revealed; and, being filled with the Holy Ghost, may learn to love and bless our persecutors.

So strengthen us by thy grace that, by the . . . constancy of our faith, even unto death, we may glorify thy name.

Grant that they may both perceive and know what things they ought to do, and also may have grace and power to faithfully fulfill the same.

In all our dangers and necessities, stretch forth thy right hand to help and defend us.

By reason of the frailty of our nature, we cannot always stand upright; grant to us such strength and protection as may support us in all dangers.

That they who do lean only upon the hope of thy heavenly grace may evermore be defended by thy mighty power.

O Lord God, who seest that we put not our trust in anything that we do; mercifully grant that by thy power we may be defended against all adversity.

Stretch forth the right hand of Thy Majesty, to be our defense against all our enemies.

Mercifully grant that we, walking in the way of the cross, may find it none other than the way of life and peace.

Grant us grace to take joyfully the sufferings of the present time, in full assurance of the glory that shall be revealed.

We humbly beseech Thee. . . . thou dost put into our

minds good desires, so by thy continual help, we may bring the same to good effect.

By thy holy inspiration we may think those things that are good, and by thy merciful guiding may perform the same.

Grant us by the same spirit to have a right judgment in all things.

That he may direct and rule us according to Thy will, comfort us in all our affections, defend us from all error and lead us into all truth.

Keep us stedfast in this faith, and evermore defend us from all adversities.

Grant that we . . . by thy mighty aid, may be defended and comforted in all dangers and adversities.

Keep us from all things that may hurt us, that we, being ready both in body and soul, may cheerfully accomplish those things which thou commandest.

The grace of God is found through desire, sacrament, service, prayer, the Bible, and sacrifice. Later on we shall evaluate the powers or virtues which can be conveyed by grace and experience. Here we are focusing on the virtues that assure both the experience of righteousness and the experience of certain victory. And these, we must note, rarely come by a cataclysmic flash. Instead, they come through the continued perseverance

29

of the Christian pilgrim who seeks to "daily increase in His spirit more and more."

When the Rev. Wilburn C. Campbell was consecrated Bishop in the Diocese of West Virginia, the preacher was Lauriston L. Scaife, Bishop of Western New York. One portion of the sermon, though brief, became lodged in my consciousness through a receptive need. His point was just this one we have been discussing: it is a man's duty to be right. And to fulfill this duty, he must practice—not half-heartedly, but whole-heartedly—dependence on God.

Bishop Scaife in his sermon also explained that a Christian must not be a man pleaser; God alone is his judge. Once a man has firmly established this belief in his heart, he is on strong ground. He then need fear no man. When this sense of rightness is indelibly imprinted in his subconscious mind; when he has found ways and means whereby he is convinced that his plan is in cooperation with the divine plan, he no longer "halts between two opinions." He is now courageous, strong, and filled with the energy of undivided conviction, while the grace of God flows through him. Though he be reviled and ridiculed, and though "ten thousand shall fall beside him," he knows that the protection of

God is around him and that he can stand firmly against the world, the flesh, and the Devil, with confident joy ringing throughout his being.

No man can be a great leader without the basic conviction that he is standing in the right. This is the faith that has lifted average and mediocre men far above themselves and has made the Washingtons, Lincolns, and Lees great figures in history. When the center of one's being is so rooted and grounded in the conviction that God and himself are agreed on a particular venture, then the whole world can turn against him, and yet he will stand firm, come what may.

A true conviction that one is standing in the right is not a matter of stubbornness but a matter of inner light, largely a gift of God's grace and thus the fruit of faith in God. Fanatics and fools appear to have this quality, but they finally disintegrate and wilt under fire. On the other hand, the world when confronted with a man who has the real thing, who has a conviction that is rooted and grounded in the Word of God, often tries to dismiss the phenomenon by calling it fanatical or emotional. But in the end the world is humbled by this most powerful virtue.

When a man is "right" within himself as a result of

31

the gift of faith provided by the grace of God, he is free from the frustrations which ultimately shatter his nerves, and which set up conflicting organic forces that finally destroy both his body and mind through the internal explosions of his emotions. When a man is really right, his health is assured until such time as God in His infinite wisdom calls him to an out-of-the-physical-body experience in Paradise. When a man is truly right, he knows within himself that by the grace of God his purpose and cause is invincible, that his soul is indestructible, and that the right will be victorious.

GREATEST ENEMY, MOST VALUED FRIEND

CHAPTER THREE

GREATEST ENEMY, MOST VALUED FRIEND

Before we start talking about the virtues which we shall seek as a gift from God, it is most important to recognize the greatest hindrance, as well as the greatest aid, toward the winning of the pearl of great price— "a right judgment in all things."

That which causes more faulty judgments than any other human failing is pride. Like many words in the English language, pride has two quite different meanings. People, as a rule, think of pride as a commendable quality. Popularly, it connotes the strong characteristics of self-reliance, independence, self-re-

35

spect, and the ability to stand on one's two feet; it also connotes the quality that prevents us from doing an unworthy act. But from the religious and theological point of view, however, the popular usage of the word is misleading. Pride, in its original sense connotes the most destructive and powerful disease that can enter into a man's consciousness. It is the vice that separates us from God.

Scholars tell us that no other religion teaches the danger of pride and the virtue of its converse, humility, as does Christianity. In this all important emphasis, Christianity is unique. Pride is vicious because it swells the human ego to the point where it rebels against God and seeks all honor and glory for itself. Pride causes human beings to set themselves above God. This leads to spiritual blindness, and therefore to vast and irreparable mistakes. Pride means that we trust only ourselves and our own judgment. The wisdom of God is no longer sought. Pride is the cause of all the great and little Hitlers, Mussolinis, and Stalins "in every city block" (as George Bernard Shaw said). In their wake follow endless destruction, disease, misery, death, and pain. Pride causes us to become unteachable and blind. Self-will, which pride creates, makes us domineering bullies

36

who lead others on to certain destruction. It is the essential meaning of the Adam and Eve story.

Pride flourishes in every walk of life—in the most polite and educated circles and in the lowest slum areas. It slips into our lives in as seemingly harmless a manner as the Communist cell slips into a nation's State Department. It is found in the hearts of those who believe themselves to be most piously devoted to religion. No character can be more obnoxious than a spiritual snob; in his case religion becomes a force dedicated to the anti-christ. You can find pride at work in almost every phase of human experience. It makes parents blindly cruel. It produces intolerant bosses, pompously stupid scientists, and despotic rulers. Those people who possess pride are often the ones who have hoodwinked themselves into believing that they are the most humble.

The minute pride enters into consciousness, it is literally impossible to have a right judgment in anything. The pride-filled person will make decisions according to his own misguided prejudices and sooner or later disaster will have its way. Pride is equally dangerous when it leads us to a trust in people as our final hope rather than in God. This causes us to put confidence in men who have convinced us that they

37

alone have the right answers to our needs and problems.

How can we help people know when they are full of this disease of the ego? It is the job of religion to encourage people to look at themselves, their actions, and their attitudes in such an objective manner that they will be able to know whether or not this deadly virus of the soul is leading them to self-destruction.

The grace of God and the teachings of Jesus Christ, and these alone, must be our possessions if we are to fight pride in ourselves. They must also be the background and standard for all our judgments if we are to relate ourselves correctly to the unfailing universal laws of God. As the psalmist says: "It is better to trust in the Lord, than to put any confidence in man." Obviously, we must trust our neighbors in the ordinary pursuance of our daily tasks, but all ultimate judgment and trust can rest only in God. We must be careful even with persons whom we believe to be truly God-centered. "Be as wise as serpents" in determining whether or not the sin of pride is motivating the actions of others when critical decisions are to be made. Continued prayer and spiritual insight will suffice if we have the patience to seek it constantly and to wait for its manifestations.

38

Jesus frequently warns us against the sin of pride in such verses as Matthew 6:5-8. "And when thou prayest, thou shalt not be as the hypocrites are: for they love to pray standing in the synagogues and in the corners of the streets, that they may be seen of men. Verily I say unto you, They have their reward. But thou, when thou prayest, enter into thy closet, and when thou hast shut thy door, pray to thy Father which is in secret; and thy Father which seeth in secret shall reward thee openly. But when ye pray, use not vain repetitions as the heathen do: for they think that they shall be heard for their much speaking. Be not ye therefore like unto them: for your Father knoweth what things ye have need of, before ye ask him."

Again in Matthew 23:5-7, Jesus says: "But all their works they do for to be seen of men: they make broad their phylacteries, and enlarge the borders of their garments, and love the uppermost rooms at feasts, and the chief seats in the synagogues, and greetings in the markets, and to be called of men, Rabbi, Rabbi."

Let us dare paraphrase this in modern terms as it may pertain to a few of us clergy. "But all their works they do to be seen of men. They complicate their sermons with theological phrases not understood by

39

the people. They worship academic hoods, gowns, and added degrees. They set themselves up above their brethren through intellectual pride and look down upon those of little education who very often possess great humility and kindness of heart. They either become so liberal that they reduce the standards of Jesus to inconsequential wishful thinking, or so dogmatic that they make God inhuman and unmerciful. They are either most punctilious in the wearing of frock coats and cutaways on Sunday morning or they wear the highest clerical collars and most sumptuous embroideries on their vestments as they pace before the altars of God. It is not that God is displeased by reverent worship, but that He is saddened when His ministers take unto themselves the glory due to Him. They want to be seated at the high table at banquets, to serve on the most influential ecclesiastical committees, and to be hailed at conventions as among the better known ecclesiastics of our time. They relish being called, 'Doctor, Doctor,' or 'Father, Father.' "

Jesus also calls attention to the sin of pride in Luke 18:9: "And he spake this parable unto certain which trusted in themselves that they were righteous, and despised others." He attacks the pride of race and tradition in Luke 3:8 when He says: "Bring forth therefore fruits worthy of repentance, and begin not to say within yourselves, We have Abraham to our father: for I say unto you, That God is able of these stones to raise up children unto Abraham."

Notice how often He makes the lowliest of persons the heroes of His parables. He chooses the most despised social outcasts to show that pride of family tree, background, or economic and social standing has nothing to do with the Kingdom of God. Note His words in the story of the Good Samaritan, how He has contrasted him with the high and mighty, the priest and Levite. "But a certain Samaritan, as he journeyed came where he was: and when he saw him, he had compassion on him, and went to him, and bound up his wounds, pouring in oil and wine, and set him on his own beast, and brought him to an inn, and took care of him. And on the morrow when he departed, he took out two pence, and gave them to the host, and said unto him, Take care of him . . . Which now of these three, thinkest thou, was neighbour unto him that fell among the thieves?" (*Luke 10:33-36*)

Christ's great emphasis is upon humility. He instructed His followers to beware of exalted positions

41

and special privilege. "But be not ye called Rabbi: for one is your Master, even Christ; and all ye are brethren. . . . But he that is greatest among you shall be your servant. And whosoever shall exalt himself shall be abased; and he that shall humble himself shall be exalted. But woe unto you, scribes and Pharisees, hypocrites! for ye shut up the kingdom of heaven against men: for ye neither go in yourselves, neither suffer ye them that are entering to go in. Woe unto you, scribes and Pharisees, hypocrites!" (*Matt. 23:8-14*)

Again in Mark He chides those who seek the important places of honor and position. "And he said unto them, What would ye that I should do for you? They said unto him, Grant unto us that we may sit, one on thy right hand, and the other on thy left hand, in thy glory. But Jesus said unto them, Ye know not what ye ask: can ye drink of the cup that I drink of? and be baptized with the baptism that I am baptized with? And they said unto him, We can. And Jesus said unto them, Ye shall indeed drink of the cup that I drink of . . . But to sit on my right hand and on my left hand is not mine to give; but it shall be given to them for whom it is prepared. And when the ten heard it, they began to be much displeased . . . whosoever of you will be

42

the chiefest, shall be servant of all. For even the Son of man came not to be ministered unto, but to minister, and to give his life a ransom for many." (*Mark 10:36-45*)

It was a significant example that Jesus set when He washed the feet of His disciples to prove to them that they must become servants of the most lowly. Thus, it was more by His life and actions than by His words that He introduced a new and great virtue—the virtue of Christian humility.

St. Paul takes the cue from Jesus and makes much of this virtue. He glories in his own weakness in order to teach that the power of the Almighty is the only force that can accomplish the great things of the Gospel he preaches. He shows that in the power of Christ he is made strong, but that of his own power he can do nothing.

The virtue of humility is a great Christian force. Through it alone can the power of Almighty God operate. Humility does not mean self-deprecation, groveling before human beings, being a Caspar Milquetoast. Humility simply means that a man does not trust in his own power to help himself. It means that he realizes that by his own strength he is inadequate but that by the power of Christ within him, he is endowed with

43

the strength and the courage and the grace through which all things can become possible. Humility means that a man will be teachable at all times and willing to seek the truth as it is presented to him, whether it hurts or not.

I witnessed an apt example of humility and teachability in the summer of 1952 when Major General John P. McConnell, Commanding General of the Strategic Air Command, Seventh Air Division, located in England, sent me on a tour of his bases. He drove me out to the airport and introduced me to Colonel White, who was to be my aide.

We drove over to the plane, a beautiful four-engine C-54, where I was introduced to the crew—pilot, radio operator, and flight engineer. For awhile after taking off, the colonel acted as copilot. Later he left the cockpit and invited me to sit in his seat at the dual controls, which I did. Before long we approached Lakenheath, our first stop. As Colonel White desired to land the ship, I gave up my seat at the controls to him and went back to sit in a bucket seat.

We came in for what I thought was a perfect landing. A young flight sergeant, bumming a ride back to his base, was sitting in a bucket seat near me. After

44

we landed, he asked, "Sir, did the colonel land the plane?" I answered in the affirmative. When the gangway was rolled up and the door opened, the sergeant stood beside his seat while the colonel, who had landed the plane, passed by. I was amazed to hear the sergeant address the colonel as follows: "Sir, you had her tail down first."

The colonel gave him a quick, stern glance and said, "What do you know about it?" The sergeant replied, "Sir, it was a smooth landing but I know you set her tail down first because I could feel it." The colonel quipped, "That was a damned good landing."

The colonel and I started down the steps. He took my arm and leaned over. Confidentially, he said, "I think the sergeant may be right." He waited for the boy at the bottom of the stairs. "Son, you're sure about that, are you?" he asked. The boy smiled and answered, "Yes, sir, I am, sir." Colonel White then asked the boy if he could help him in any way. Could he take him to his barracks, or could he give him a lift? The boy declined, thanked him for the ride, and went on his way.

Two days later I dined with General McConnell and told him the story. He laughed heartily and said, "That's pretty good. The sergeant wears wings, and

45

while he is not a pilot, we count him as a pro; and we try to encourage him to have confidence in his own judgment. Furthermore, as a member of a crew, he can criticize any man that flies as long as he does it with respect and discipline."

I added that I felt Colonel White was very humble and tolerant in the way he took the joshing. The general said, "Good combat aircrews are made by training, but *great* combat crews are made by training and honest criticism. The mere fact that each crew member does his work under the observation of others goes a long way toward the achievement of perfection."

I wonder how many of us who "profess and call ourselves Christians" and work in the Lord's vineyard can take criticism as humbly as that colonel of the United States Air Force, who placed humility and the job requirements above pride, rank, and the love of authority?

THE TRUTH SHALL MAKE YOU FREE

CHAPTER FOUR

THE TRUTH SHALL MAKE YOU FREE

In discussing the position of truth as it relates to "right judgment," we shall start with a negative danger and work toward positive accomplishment.

We need to be extremely careful when we use the word truth; the slightest abuse may cause us to slip into the hideous sin of self-righteousness. When someone believes that he has the truth on his side, he must have the accompanying will (as we noted in the first chapter) to see all the truth available. If he does not possess this openness, he is likely to become unwittingly the enemy of the virtue he claims to own.

49

Our Lord was especially hard on the self-righteous Pharisee because He was convinced of His own piety and, consequently, was impossible to teach. This happens to many modern Christians. We profess and call ourselves Christians, are good Episcopalians, or Methodists, or Roman Catholics, or Presbyterians. We know our rituals, our ecclesiastical theories, our historical points of pride; we are so familiar with the things that relate to God, that we mistake them for a personal God-relationship. More often than not, the hardest people to convert are "good churchmen." They are like the man who stood in the temple and prayed with gratitude to God that he was not like other men, while the poor publican, not daring to lift his eyes, asked God to be merciful to him a sinner. In many instances, the people most in need of conversion are those who think they are converted. It was ever thus, for the converted are blinded through their own self-righteousness.

"Let him who is without sin among you cast the first stone."

Time and again our Lord lashed out against the self-righteous. We, who belong to this group, are usually the first to cast stones. Most of us have moments of disservice in this category. Our Lord continues to preach this sermon down through the ages, and whenever we profess to be good churchmen or are tempted to criticize without understanding, we can be likened unto those who charged the woman with adultery and took up stones to cast upon her. Jesus is continually preaching this one-sentence sermon to every unsuspecting self-righteous individual, and His saying, "He who is without sin among you, let him first cast a stone at her" (*John 5:7*), applies at one time or another to every one of us.

The self-righteous are usually blinded by their own sincerity. Sincerity alone is doubtful proof of a right judgment. Many sincere people are among the most misguided. Bishop Irving P. Johnson, of Colorado, used to say that he was always afraid of sincere people. He said that the most sincere man he ever knew was in an insane asylum. He was completely convinced that he was Napoleon.

Hitler, no doubt, was sincere. He was sure that it was his high and destined calling to rid Germany of the Jews. It made no difference to him how the millions of suffering Israelites were liquidated. Often he lost himself in mystical reverie by listening to great arias from Wagnerian operas. On such occasions he would become

51

so inspired that he could rise up and use his new found mystical inspiration as the source of energy to initiate ever greater evil deeds. Look carefully at sincerity; first you must plumb its depths to see if it is based on the great virtues pertaining to the love of Christ.

In seeking to develop the gift of right judgment, it is highly important that we examine our approaches to everyday disagreements and controversies. Are we among those who are always convinced that they are right on almost every issue? Yes, we may reply that we are fair—but are we? The world is full of people who prefer to have almost any catastrophe happen rather than to admit either that they are wrong or that they have made a mistake in judgment or action. Many of us reading these sentences will thank God that we are not such men—yet, are we not? Ask someone very close to you how many times he has heard you make an honest apology or an admission of wrongdoing. How many of us who profess and call ourselves Christians are openly penitent when necessary? Some of us, both bishops and clergy, lead the pack; and thus, in the name of Christianity, we all too often represent the anti-christ. The ABC of Christianity is a desire for humility, whereby we may know the truth about ourselves, joined with the grace to admit our bad judgments quickly when we are wrong.

Modern man is a great seeker of the truth in almost every field of endeavor, save that which concerns his own prejudices, hatreds, and weaknesses. We give millions, even billions, to the goddesses of education, science, and the arts. Foundations build up vast sums of money that can be tapped at almost any moment for the building of a new cyclotron, for research in literature, for archeology, or for any of the other fields that relate to intellectual pursuits. When it comes to spiritual research into the truth about one's own soul, however, we are all too frequently warned that it is subjective and dangerous. Yet, it is not possible to build a good society that does not believe in healthy research into man's individual foibles or into the lies by which man fools himself. Until a man faces himself with his God, he is a potential menace to society.

For years I have made it a hobby to read all the books I can find on Ignatius Loyola, the founder of the Jesuits, and John Wesley, the founder of the Methodists. It is amazing to find that these two great religious leaders—two of the greatest since the days of Paul— were so much alike in a variety of characteristics. One of the virtues each possessed was the willingness to seek the truth about himself. They did not leap to every criticism that came from the swarms of enemies that surrounded them, but when a serious accusation was brought to their attention, it was always given consideration. Both were filled with humble gratitude if shown that one of their conclusions was based on a false premise. Loyola and Wesley gave thanks with great humility to the lowliest person who pointed out a shortcoming.

Christianity in our time should start from a study of God-given qualities as seen in unspoiled children and teach people that a willing desire to know the truth about themselves is the first of the virtues, for without it there can be no Christian faith. The Church as a whole, and I include all divisions and denominations, is today reeking with spiritual pride, self-righteousness, and inner blindness. There are none so blind as those who refuse to see!

All the brilliance of modern theology, all the ingenious ability of the higher critics of the Bible, all the marvels of liturgical art, all the beauty of liturgical music, all the wonders of church architecture—all these are useless and mean absolutely nothing if those who

54

are absorbed in them cannot seek and know the truth about themselves.

Yet, when we seek the truth about ourselves let us watch that we do not become violently discouraged and hopelessly depressed. As the ego-deflating truth is perceived, there must simultaneously be taught the loving kindness and tender mercy of the Father, "whose property is always to have mercy." Abhorrent to Him as sin must be, He forgives time after time, time after time. He is so aware of our human frailties and weaknesses that we can have hope in spite of our continued mistakes, if we believe in the wonderful power of His forgiveness.

Psychiatrists are right when they warn us of the devastating and destructive power of a sense of guilt. Christianity takes care of that, for a loving Father is continually standing by to forgive us again and again when we are willing to face the truth about ourselves and ask Him to give us a clean heart and His blessing. He never fails to take our sins, when we are truly penitent, and incorporate them, forgiven by his mercy, into a new and rich pattern of life for us.

When we begin to want the truth and joyfully receive His forgiveness, then will we be well on the way

55

toward ridding ourselves of self-righteousness; then we are on the way toward attaining Christ's power for "a right judgment in all things." Furthermore, we shall be teachable because we are growing in childlike humility.

AN ANALOGY WITH A TWIST

CHAPTER FIVE

AN ANALOGY WITH A TWIST

An interesting feature of the Gospel is the way in which its wisdom comes upon us with shocking surprise. The so called practical philosophy of the ordinary man is frequently the opposite of the wise teachings of our Lord. Man's reasoning is based upon the experience of a perishable materialism, while our Lord's values come straight from universal spiritual law.

We tend, for example, to say that if a man wants to get ahead in life, he should move out in front, stay there and beat off the rest of the pack who try to dislodge him. Our Lord tells us that if we want to arrive at truth and peace and right judgment (for without these we have anxiety, distress, ulcers, and no taste for being out in front should we get there), we have to begin at the tail end and be last. Man says that charity begins at home and that if we do not look out for ourselves first, no one else will. Our Lord says that we can never find our life and be redeemed until we have lost our life in God —a cause greater than our self.

Many of us who have social ambitions are convinced that if we are to get ahead, we must be sure to make the right contacts and have the best connections. Our Lord tells us to take the lowest seat and first to become servants of all before we can be lifted into any kind of prominence. To our earthly way of thinking, we believe that we ought to amass all the money we can lay hand to and build a fortune, but our Lord tells us that in order to have a nonperishable fortune, we must give until it hurts and then, only, will we receive true riches.

When it comes to wisdom and right judgment, the worldly minded send people to wise old heads who have had plenty of earthly experience. That is not the way our Lord approached it, for He told us that the best judgment will come when we study the simple and

60

instinctive reactions of a child. In Matthew 18:2, He says: "Except ye be converted and be as little children, ye shall not enter into the Kingdom of Heaven. Whosoever therefore shall humble himself as this little child, the same is the greatest in the Kingdom of Heaven." In other words, the more we desire to grow wiser in making our long-term decisions, the more humble we have to be, so that our attitudes will be simple and direct. If we want to increase in the ability to live strong and healthy lives, we must decrease our egocentric reactions. Therefore, our search for relief from frustration, worry, anxiety, nervous breakdowns, and other adult troubles leads us to the humbling teaching of our Lord—that we can learn from little children.

The principal reason why a little child invariably steals the show is that he has not yet been taught to be self-conscious. He is a free-moving and free-acting agent who does not perform for applause or mug for the center of the camera. You are never sure what he will do next or how he will express himself, but you are confident that whatever movement he makes will be a spontaneous surprise. Thus, you watch him with fascination, and he is superb as long as he does not know he has an audience or what an audience means.

61

Recently, I watched a little child, hardly able to walk, tumble and splash and creep and walk about in a shallow wading pool. He was utterly without self-consciousness, and when he fell, he seemed to think it was a huge joke, even though the water splashed into his laughing eyes and open mouth. Soon there was a crowd surrounding him, watching his capers in sheer delight. No actor could possibly compete with this tiny scene-stealer. You cannot beat naturalness.

Should that same child, however, be taught by his fascinated elders to repeat the performance for applause and approval, he would cease to be a delightful free spirit and change into an objectionable little show-off. The attention, the praise, and the baby-talk prattle of his adult admirers, who would constantly coax repeat performances, would make him self-conscious with a "How'm I doin', Ma" attitude. The unself-consciousness of natural children can be ruined in a short time by the stupidity of grownups. Their instinctive God-given charm can soon be lost, and they can become boring ham actors.

Many of us grow up to be brats who live for approval and applause. When we reach the stage of audience awareness, we acquire the malady of the "what-will-people-think" motivation. This causes us to perform for the shallow praise of men, and means we are not motivated by the judgment of God; it brings us to that terrifying condition wherein we can no longer be trusted for a "right judgment" in anything. We will sellout our most trusted friends and beloved benefactors should we feel that by being seen with them, some particular group will disapprove or ridicule us. We will sellout principle, standards, and those whom we profess to love the most for the cheap approval of people who have not the character to appreciate value.

To undo our years of training in self-consciousness calls for us to pray to become as uncomplex as a little child whose motives are unmixed. To be free from the opinions of fickle men and women and to care only for the joy of pleasing God are two of the true thrills of the Christian life, for "in His service is perfect freedom."

Let us visualize this picture. Our Lord is asked certain questions about the Kingdom of Heaven by His disciples. He replies by calling a little child into the center of the group and seating him "in the midst of

63

them," the youngster assuming the high position of teacher. In our present sophisticated world, it is hard to see any wisdom in this action. We are puzzled by it, but it challenges us. Must we always turn only to wise old heads and assume that we can learn nothing from children? Or shall we be humble and see what it is that we can learn from a child? Shall we change our attitude, try the latter, and see if the profound wisdom of the gospel does not come as a shocking surprise?

In Matthew, Jesus is talking about a very small child and wants to teach his disciples the qualities a man of right judgment will have. He does not select a child corrupted and spoiled by a too-close contact with the selfish actions of practical men. The child that Jesus must be talking about has God-given traits that are as yet untainted by the stumbling and bumbling of adults. The child's natural, instinctive, unspoiled reactions are object lessons for the disciples and for us. And until the worldly-wise adult regains such qualities as childlike faith, dependence, imagination, wonder, spontaneity, unself-consciousness, and flexibility, he cannot possess the spiritual stature from which will issue right judgments in all things.

64

THE PROFOUND WAY OF A LITTLE CHILD

CHAPTER SIX

THE PROFOUND WAY
OF A LITTLE CHILD

It would be easy to become sentimental about small children and idealize them to the point of idolatry. We must try to avoid this. Our objective is not to worship the child as a child. He has little or no responsibility for those virtues we want to point out. Our objective is to admire the wisdom of God who placed such childlike qualities as humility, spontaneity, unself-consciousness, imagination, flexibility, wonder, and so forth in human nature in the first place. It is these natural character-istics of divine origin that we would observe, always realizing, of course, that their perfect blossoming is never achieved even in a child. Too early are the child's God-like traits poisoned and corrupted by the bad examples of older people.

In this chapter and the next we will focus upon God's marks of wisdom as He put them in the child and attempt to illustrate how their repossession can be applied to adult needs. We are sure that these marks of wisdom provide laws of living which will save us from many false choices and much unnecessary suffering. Our problem will be to believe that they work better than our own cynical and misguided habits which for the most part send us on from blunder to blunder.

When the Christ told us to study the little child for entrance requirements to the Kingdom of Heaven, He did not expect us to become involved in a technical discussion of child psychology. On the contrary, it was the unspoiled God-given traits of childhood that he wanted us to observe—not the child's intelligence quotient (IQ) or his undeveloped motor responses. Should we miss this point in His analogy, we may miss the full significance of His teaching. Instead of focusing on the child as a reflection of God's wisdom, we may be led into the detailed research of experimental and labora-

68

tory science. This is an important area, but it has little to do with our search for avenues to right judgment.

Nevertheless, in order not to find ourselves in conflict with any findings of science that may overlap our search, we have gone to an internationally known baby and child authority. We have studied with great interest and with special care Dr. Benjamin Spock's important book, *Baby and Child Care*. We must be aware as we look for the native traits of innate wisdom and instinctive right judgment in children of the truth that child character traits differ, and differ sometimes radically, at various stages of early growth. Dr. Spock points this out as fact: a trait true about one child one month may be radically altered the next. With this as proper admonition, let us now see what a child can teach each and every one of us.

A little child is utterly dependent upon his parents and is instinctively aware of it. Without parental care, he is helpless. Whenever he has a need, he makes a noise and goes on making it until some kind of relief arrives. All food, shelter, clothing, and care must be provided because, of himself, he can do nothing for himself. When he grows large enough and adventuresome enough to start out on his two knees or two feet alone and proceeds to get into trouble, he bellows, and scrambles back to his mother for security and her parental protection.

The real Christian never outgrows an analogous sense of utter dependence. He transfers it from mother and father to God the Creator and Provider of all life, energy, and sustenance. Not unlike the child, the Christian knows that he needs extra power outside himself to meet the great troubles he faces. He knows that he cannot solve his own problems independently from divine wisdom and strength. He realizes that apart from God no strength, power, or life exists.

Modern man strives for independence, individualism, and self-sufficiency. In a way this is good, but unless one understands the true meaning and implication, it spells certain disaster. If such striving is to be really worth the effort, it must be rooted in a prior dependence on God and in a sense of awe and wonder at His mighty acts.

When I was rector of a parish, we often had parties for the children that included entertainment by a magician. It was a rare sight to watch the expressions on the faces of the littlest children who sat on the benches in the front row on such occasions. Their uninhibited emotions, their simplicity, their ready reactions, and their native desire to believe was powerfully impressive. The older boys, who sat in the back rows, were usually "wise guys" by that time, and their chief joy was to be skeptical in order to expose the magician. Of course, the magician anticipated the "wise guys" and allowed their doubts to play into the hands of his showmanship. The little ones, however, believed with open mouths and wide open eyes as the entertainer tapped his topper and, with a wand, turned the hat upside down. His arms were exposed; his sleeves were rolled up to the elbows. He made flourishes with his hands, and then, wonder of wonders he pulled a live rabbit out of the hat. At that point, everybody believed. But the little ones squealed with delight, faith, awe, and wonder.

When we can no longer thrill to the works of God with faith, awe, wonder, and delight, religion can do very little for us and we can do very little for religion. But God, today, can pull amazing rabbits out of our hats. Prayer, faith, and grace can change situations, conditions, and circumstances. Today, *right now,* God can redeem us from situations in which our own selfishness or the carelessness and selfishness of other people have led us.

Neale Morgan, a young clergyman, in the Diocese of Pittsburgh, related a case history of his little nephew who was run over by an automobile in New York at the age of two. Later, I read the same account in a magazine.

The child was struck at the base of his brain. Six doctors were in attendance at the hospital, including three neuro-surgeons. From the medical and scientific standpoint, it was considered a hopeless situation. He was living from minute to minute and could not be expected to pull through the night. The blow causing the concussion was to the occipital bone where all nerve centers lie. The medical men did not dare operate. The mother approached a few friends who believed strongly in prayer healing; she herself had recently joined such a prayer group. The rector, a man of great faith, came to the hospital immediately. He anointed the boy. Strong praying groups and members of classes in personal religion were enlisted. Within a few hours, over one hundred people of faith were surrounding the child with God's healing and loving presence. The first miracle that happened was that the temperature, which had risen to staggering heights, went down and life hung on through the night.

Neale's nephew continued to live from one day to the next, being unconscious for the first six days and in a state of semi-consciousness for weeks. The right eye from the beginning was given up for lost because it was terribly cut. All speech was lost, and the right side was paralyzed. It was said that if he lived, he would never walk and that he would be mentally retarded. The nerve which supplied the good eye was so damaged that he lost its vision. The doctors said that in all probability it would be necessary to remove the eye.

Life continued to hang on, however, and the prayer groups continued to pray daily. After weeks of care, with three nurses in daily attendance, the boy was taken home, helpless, with flopping arms, head, and legs. At first, he improved slowly but then, with great rapidity. Today, he is ninety-five per cent healed and romps and plays with healthy normal reactions.

In addition to awe, wonder, and dependence, a little child has native faith. He has an instinctive need and will to believe.

After speaking on this theme at St. Stephen's Church, in Sewickley, Pennsylvania, and inviting comments and suggestions, I received this letter from Mr. Walter I. Floyd:

It occurred to me after thinking back on your sermon that one of the qualities inherent in all children is faith, and whereas this is somewhat tied in with the first feature you mentioned in your talk (namely, dependence), I believe it bears consideration. A child's faith is developed through his parents, and until this child is deceived or his parents become inconsistent, his great capacity for faith develops and grows. However, note the severe letdown and disillusionment when a child's faith is suddenly shattered by a parent who is not consistent or who has deceived a child.

My thinking on the subject is that this tremendous faith which is inherent in little children can be directed to God during their development and, since God never deceives any of us nor ever lets us down, this faith can grow to tremendous proportions throughout our lifetime.

Mr. Floyd's observations point to a truth that should be underlined and stressed in Christian education. A child grows up to be as happy and secure as his faith, and the quality of his faith largely depends on the trustworthiness of his parents. Religious education for good or ill, thus, begins with the parents. The young

74

child acts on the assumption that his parents are dependable and that they will do exactly what they say they will do. He does not question, rationalize, or debate with his mother and father (and obviously he cannot) but instinctively proceeds to live by their words and deeds with complete security until they prove otherwise.

The unswerving trust of the innate faith that a child has is the trait that Jesus would teach to us. The quality of the faith that an adult should have must be analogous to that of a little child. This, when spelled out, means that the great principles of our Lord must be accepted as true until proved otherwise. Specifically, this means that we should study the teachings of our Lord in the Sermon on the Mount and elsewhere and through prayer proceed to ask for the spiritual strength to put them to the test. When we have proved that the practice of love, humility, generosity, truth, trust and patience are the most practical way of living, we are secure and convinced. Until we have proved them, we should seek the grace to act on the assumption that they point out the most sensible way to live. Thus, we become as little children and trust the words of the Father. Our Lord tells us that if the program does not work, have done with it—for if the tree does not produce fruit, chop it down. You must prove Him by practicing His program. Just as the child takes the word of his parents, or the college student takes the word of the professor, or the patient takes the prescription of the doctor, or the traveler assumes the road map is correct, so the Christian accepts and tries out (proves) the teachings of Christ.

When a Christian desires intellectual proof of God's being and existence, it is a worthy effort. But that is not really the way toward Christian faith. The adult who wants to enjoy the redemption and security of the Christian faith must become, in his trust, as a little child. The adult can know God when he tries and proves Him by acting on the assumption that the great spiritual lessons of the Bible are true and actually work in human existence. He can theorize and intellectualize about them, but until he tries to live by them, he will never really know whether they are true or false. Is God dependable? You can find out by trusting in His word and acting upon it. He tells you to "prove all things" including Himself and invites you to "taste and see how gracious the Lord is."

If we have a dependence on and faith in God

analogous to the dependence on and faith in parents that a child has, God can come to us and save us from our selfishness and egocentricity. And He can save us in amazing ways. Sometimes the redemption comes as a total surprise in the form of a release from worry or a release from some personal anxiety or frustration. Sometimes the release is not immediate, and because we need the experience, He first makes us go through pain and suffering and great difficulties. But if we honestly seek Him, He gives us power that we cannot create "of ourselves" and carries us into the face of the most trying pain, and beyond it to victory. In either case, it is the power of God that does the work. What we need is the grace to be as the little children in the front row who in faith look with awe, wonder, and delight at the wizardry of the great magician. Without this—as we look to God—there is very little power or joy in religion, and the main avenue to right judgment is closed.

GOD GAVE THESE GIFTS

CHAPTER SEVEN

GOD GAVE THESE GIFTS

God intended man to have free will and to stand up for personal freedom. Let us notice how God made even a little child a protestant against tyranny of any kind, collective or personal.

In writing about free will in a little child, Dr. Spock has this to say: "When you suggest something that doesn't appeal to him, he feels he must assert himself. His nature tells him to. He just says 'No' in words or action—even about things he likes to do. . . . Stop and think what would happen if he never felt like saying 'No.' He'd become a robot. You would be unable to resist the temptation to boss him all the time and he would stop learning and developing. When he was old

81

enough to go out into the world . . . everybody else would take advantage of him."[1]

Now consider your own sense of freedom. You were born to be free. This was God's intention, and scientists, such as Dr. Spock, point out its practical value for little children. Do you fear any man or woman? If so, you are not free. Does someone bully, dominate, nag, or press you in big or little things with undue constancy? Just remember that God did not make you for the purpose of being browbeaten by any human being. Yet, the amount of browbeating and bullying that goes on all about us in home, office, school, and wherever human beings live, one with another, is simply amazing. If you are an underdog, you are not pleasing God by docile submission. There is nothing sacred, holy, or spiritual about subservience.

Of course, you must submit to those in official authority over you in school, in business, and in the Armed Forces, or wherever some regimentation is an accepted necessity in a democratic way of life. But this is discipline of a healthy form and it is not what I am talking

---

[1] Benjamin Spock, *Common Sense Book of Baby and Child Care* (New York: Duell). Copyright 1945, 1946 by Spock. Used by permission.

about. I refer to personal relationships in which we are dominated by someone—a tyrant or a bully or a selfish family jailer. At birth you were given both the capacity to be a free individual under God and the obligation to fear none other than the Almighty. The more we allow a husband, a wife, a child, or a friend to dominate us, the more we are defying the law of the Lord in human nature and the more we let him or her get away with it, the more we are contributing (as we shall see later) to the sin of that tyrant.

A study of the child reminds us that we were born to be free. It also reminds us of the adventurous spontaneity that by nature belongs to every human being. A little child is free to be impulsive and spontaneous until such time as we smother him with "be carefuls" and "don'ts." Then he begins to be inhibited, and later on many of us parents can trace our children's problems to this smothering process. Obviously, we must inhibit children from touching such things as hot stoves, for we do not want them to get needlessly burned. But the inhibiting program administered by the average parent just builds invisible bands of repression over the child's God-given spirit of spontaneity, and that is a sad, though unconscious, kind of spiritual sabotage.

83

A little child delights us because his spontaneity is so innocent and impulsive. Sometimes he gets into trouble, but if allowed to adventure within reason, you cannot say that he does not have a good time. We tend to train the best of this quality out of him just as quickly as possible. Consequently, when the child grows up, he becomes the average respectable adult: cautious, calculating, and conservative. He is changed into a tragically bound-up conformist, conditioned to restrict most of his best impulses through fear of public opinion or through fear of losing his grasp on the trifling things of this world that have become his selfish possessions.

The secret of the right use of the spontaneous and impulsive sense of adventure rests on motive. When the heart of a man seeks honestly to know and do the will of God, when his will is guided by the Holy Spirit, he will make few mistakes acting on his best impulse. This, however, is not to say that we should live a life of unbridled, impulsive responses. We grant that much of the time we must act before we have ample opportunity to reason and that, at other times, it may be wise to act on strong impulse in spite of what seems to be good reasoning. Nevertheless, if we have always practiced a search for God's will, our motive will be "right"

84

and the actions that flow from it will be more free from mistakes than we have the right to expect.

One of the reasons our Lord loved impulsive Peter was that he was not congealed by caution but often drove ahead with an impulsive spirit of adventure. Again, the woman who spontaneously poured expensive ointment on the feet of Jesus and was roundly criticized by the cautious calculators of Jerusalem was praised by our Lord. She saw with great acuteness an opportunity that might never come again. He commended her for taking advantage of it, while it was there waiting. She has gone down in history, remembered for her spirit of adventure, a spirit that sprang out of her faith in Christ.

Adventurous action in the name of Christ can be misguided, and at times it is not without dangerous implications. It was Studdert-Kennedy who once said that Christians must be good gamblers, for we are called to bet our lives on our Lord by trusting in Him. The Christian who is not afraid to act at times on his highest impulse is usually protected, and God blesses his mistakes by making up the differences in the long run. Obviously, this means that we must always be ready to take constructive criticism and to seek the truth

85

about our shortcomings. Headlong obstinacy and self-righteousness should never be mistaken for the leading of the Holy Spirit. A life bathed in honest prayer and faithful attention to the various means of grace provided by the Church will get enough right answers to nullify the mistakes.

I do not mean to hold up Bishop Campbell of West Virginia as a paragon of Christian virtue for he is as given to mistakes as any of us, but here is what seems to me a good story of impulsive action and adventure. After returning from a trip to Korea, I was requested by the Bishop of Johannesburg, in South Africa, to select an American bishop to go to South Africa to preach a mission in this hot spot of racial tension. A number of men had been invited, and each in turn had declined. The adventure was not without dynamite. My thought went to Bishop Campbell. I telephoned him, confident of what he would say. I quickly outlined the job, what it called for, and asked for an immediate answer. It came back by return voice with two words: "Sure, when?" He was on his way within six weeks.

In addition to free will and spontaneity, one of the most wonderful qualities about a little child is the simple use to which he can put his vivid imagination. Turn him loose in the attic or in an old storeroom or on the village dump and he will come up with damaged and castoff things that to us seem useless. These he will proceed to play with for hours. The legs of a broken chair may become the center poles of a circus tent, or a torn Japanese fan may be turned into an airplane. The most depleted junk can be transformed into cherished symbols to which the child becomes attached for days and months on end.

Such a process can happen to any child because God places in each one the standard equipment of an excellent imagination. As Paul says, "We come behind in no gift."

Now what do we adults do? We spoil this priceless endowment by not encouraging the child to use it. We buy costly toys and elaborate gadgets and shower him with them so that he grows bored before he can learn to enjoy them. We give a little boy an expensive electric train which he cannot possibly appreciate because it is far too advanced for him. Furthermore, from whistle to caboose it personifies and does everything he wants to personify and do for himself. The train makes the whistle noises he wants to make, and it runs automatically—a process of little interest to one still in the creeping and pushing stage. Instead of the train, what he needs is a wooden block that may not even closely resemble an engine. He can push, pull, and toot a set of blocks, but an expensive train can only be run when Papa is home. With Papa's train, all the active little fellow can do is sit on the side lines and be an audience. Papa, of course, has the fun.

The child has a "whopper" of an imagination and a great sense of adventure within himself, if we will turn him loose on simple playthings and give his imagination a chance to operate. He will develop a sense of discovery that will grow in him all of his life. To orient this same imagination to the realm of religion, will mean adventure of unlimited proportions.

It is interesting to note how many grownups have convinced themselves that they are devoid of the gift of imagination. Everyone has the gift. All the more reason, then, why we should return to some of the attitudes of the child. If you do not believe you have a creative imagination, let me ask you if you ever have any fears. Analyze fear. What is it but the projection of this great quality of imagination! It deals with things in the future, and these are imagined projections because they have not yet occurred. Who is devoid of fear? Who is devoid of imagination?

Watch a child sit in a chair and pretend he is a pilot in a jet, a G-man with a machine gun, a space ship captain, a world series pitcher, or a hundred other wonders he can create. What child cannot use his fantastic imagination in wondrous ways if he is given a chance. You personally have the same equipment and it can be turned to healthy and useful hobbies and to all kinds of projects, your business included. It is not necessary for you to go to Bermuda or to Mexico or on a North Cape cruise or to spend large portions of your income in keeping up with the Joneses. Simple fun built on your imagination is far more rewarding. (I suggest you read Alex Osborne's book, *Your Creative Power*, for further general thoughts on this theme.)

The complex skepticism of the adult is what stands in the way of the imaginative simplicity expressed by little children. It is difficult for the cautious sophisticate to believe in the spiritual world that the Church has always claimed to be about us. True, you cannot prove that the world of the unseen exists objectively and yet,

89

proof may come through the study being made in the field of extrasensory perception and fostered today at many reputable universities throughout the world. However, we do have vast amounts of evidence of the power of the unseen world of the spirit as related to the spiritual experience of millions of people over a span of hundreds of years.

One of the most comforting doctrines of the Church is that of the Communion of Saints. This teaches that we can be and are in close touch with "angels, archangels, and the whole company of heaven." Those of us who believe in these hosts of friends hold that they are assigned to give spiritual assistance to the people of the earth. We are greatly helped by the conviction that we can call on them at any time and will receive immediate help.

Furthermore, we believe that we can pray for the departed in Paradise just as realistically as if they were in the flesh. We are convinced that the departed can also pray for us and actually give us greater assistance in the unseen realm than they could when they were on earth. We believe that the unseen hosts can now observe life on earth from a new dimension. They have a new vision of what is important and can be of incalculable assistance to us. After one has believed and prayed with them, one gets a sense of their presence and surrounding comfort which cannot come to us from any other source or in any other manner. It is sad to see how few Christians, including the clergy, I fear, actually believe in and use this great teaching.

Asking the aid of the great saints of the past is also an invaluable asset to the practical life we ought to live today. Realize that the mystics and the saints throughout the ages have always been hard-headed, practical men who organized vast societies of people in dedicated bands of cooperative Christians. When we invoke the aid of the saints, it does not mean that we are praying to them as to lesser gods. It means that we are respecting them as persons of rich experience and spiritual insight (which the world so desperately needs) and enlisting their aid and their prayers. To the little child, the unseen world is real, wonderful, and comfortable. He makes friends with angels easily, and they play with him and protect him. If we are not afraid to teach the little child the power of this unseen companionship, we will find that, with simple and imaginative faith, they will take to this powerful tradition of the Christian Church and correspondingly benefit from it all the rest of their lives.

To those of you who have sons or husbands or loved ones who fly for the Armed Forces, I would covet no greater comfort for you than to pray daily for them by calling upon the unseen saints to protect and sustain them. I am sure that our unseen hosts take a great many of the flying boys through some terribly tight spots.

It is surprising how wonderfully helpful in forming right judgments in Christ, relationships with the unseen are. It is my belief that somehow they communicate wisdom, timing, balance, and spiritual hunches which through faith we are able to use constructively. Obviously, I am not advocating mediumistic spiritualism but rather the straight truths that come from the Bible and the Book of Common Prayer. When one begins to see this unlimited realm of aid, one begins to live in a new and a powerful and a friendly world held together through the power of the Blessed Trinity.

For your own sake, then, pray for the simple, imaginative faith of a child.

92

LOVE THY NEIGHBOR

CHAPTER EIGHT

LOVE THY NEIGHBOR

Dr. Spock calls our attention to a trait in a small child which, in an adult, is an absolutely indispensable virtue if our relationships with other people are to be redeeming and truly Christian, and if our judgments are to be respected and reliable. It is a characteristic our Lord advocated in these words: "Be angry and sin not."

The doctor tells us that when a little child is thwarted, punished, or angered by a parent or an older person, he does not react with personal hate or resentment. Dr. Spock says this, "When he's thwarted he knows it, and feels angry. Yet he doesn't usually attack

95

the parent who has interfered with him. . . . When the feeling of fury boils up in him, he can't think of anything better to do than take it out on the floor and himself. He flops down, yelling, and pounds with his hands and feet and maybe his head."[1] I recall our jet fighter pilot son when he was a little fellow. He then showed all the instincts of fury that made him quite a baby-battler. He used to fight the floor and throw things and make ominous noises which sounded like an infuriated diamond-back rattler. But not until he was old enough to copy our bad example did he get angry and want to pound us.

Thus, the little child tends to have a virtue which, if he could maintain or recapture it for the rest of his life, would save him from future unhappiness, pain, and physical illness. Personal hate, resentment, recrimination, retaliation and jealousy—when directed toward another person—turn into psychopathic poisons. They affect our judgments and render them unreliable. They affect our glands and throw them into unbalanced operation, either over- or under-producing in their func-

---

[1] Benjamin Spock, *Common Sense Book of Baby and Child Care* (New York: Duell, Sloan and Pearce), p. 255. Copyright 1945, 1946 by Benjamin Spock. Used by permission of the publisher.

tions and therefore destroying our lives, socially and physically.

If we can pray for the grace to view all human relationships impersonally (in the sense I shall describe in a minute) and can develop an impersonal philosophy, we can save ourselves untold suffering. Furthermore, if we can find impersonal outlets for our fury, we can let off much of the steam that so easily causes us to get burned. Outlets, such as bellowing aloud in private, throwing things (which noisily crash without serious damage), walking it off, beating a drum (my outlet), or opening other valves that will relieve us, tend to be a wonderful solution. But to let anger burn inside with deliberate and guided animosity toward our fellow human beings is fatal.

When you can look at every man with the point of view of what God intended him to become rather than from the viewpoint of what he is at any given moment, you can begin to live the impersonal life. This is relatively easy for me to say, but most difficult for me to exercise at certain moments. Nevertheless, we as Christians, must strive to separate the sin from the sinner if we are to have any semblance of inner peace. Furthermore, we will seek to believe that every man is a child of God, that the Kingdom of God is within all people, and that we can identify God in us with God in them.

This does not mean that we are to be easygoing with bullies and let them abuse us or others. This is a sin against the abuser as well as against ourselves. We must stand up for our normal rights and freedoms as persons. God has instructed us to fear no man, and He has called us to perfect freedom. We must speak out and act when right principle is involved, but the secret is to do it with strength and vigor against the injustice rather than against the person.

We can take a fine, high fidelity record player as an example. The instrument is, in itself, a wonderful mechanism, capable of rendering the very best of music played by the finest of symphony orchestras in the world. We place ten records on the spindle, but by mistake a bad one has crept in among them. It is warped and full of scratches. All goes well until the concert is interrupted by this hideous record. We jump to the machine in protest, stop it, and take off the bad record. Our anger is directed at that which comes from the loudspeaker, and our objective is to stop it quickly. We do not hate the machine or the instrument or the

98

speaker, do we? We do not destroy it with the nearest ax. What we do is crack the record over our knee and throw it in the wastebasket so that it can never be replayed.

With the human instrument and the unpleasant record it plays, you cannot be so concrete. You can, however, develop a point of view that approximates the record player. You can love the instrument God made and attack the record he is playing by prayer, kindness, and protestant action if necessary.

The Bible states that next to loving God, the highest virtue is to love your neighbor, and this can easily and naturally be developed in a child if we do not spoil him. The child, says Dr. Spock, "smiles easily because he is a social being . . . He already knows that he is a sociable being, that it is nice to have loving people around, that he feels like responding to them. And if he is treated with plenty of affection and not too much interference, he will go on being friendly and reasonable, just because it is his nature."[2]

When old enough to wander out into the front yard, John wants to be a friendly little fellow and will play with whatever child comes along. His new neigh-

[2] *Ibid.*, p. 255.

99

bor or transient friend may be a little Negro or a China-man or Mohammedan or Jew or Gentile but that makes no difference. He sees a child who wants to play with him and get acquainted, and if we let them alone, they will become fast friends. Discrimination, racial preju-dice, and social superiority are taught by us adults. We prepare the way for social and racial and religious war by our bitter attitudes of hate and pride. If we have them, the child will learn them, no matter how we try to coat them over in his presence. There can be no true Christianity without a sense of love for all sorts and conditions of men regardless of race, color, or creed. The fact is that God created all of us, and within each, regardless of station or race, He placed "the light that lighteth every man that cometh into the world." The spark of His own Being is in all humanity, and to dis-criminate against any one of His creatures is to discrim-inate against God Himself.

This does not mean that we can like all people equally (that is literally impossible) or that we have not the right to choose our own personal friends or that our tastes must be lowered to the common denominator of all men. Love means that we must practice absolute fairness in giving opportunity to every man who honestly seeks to work; it means that we can not feel superior to any of God's creatures; it means that we judge and accept a man solely on the basis of his character and willingness to be taught; it means that as Christians we believe that we are called to serve and to do "good unto all men and especially to those that are of the household of faith." Furthermore, love means that we will serve, sacrifice, and fight for the just rights of men.

The Christian gospel also means that we will always seek to aid those people that are the most despised by their fellowmen. The Rev. L. M. Charles-Edwards, Vicar of St. Martin-in-the Fields, London, preached in my cathedral in Pittsburgh several years ago and told the story of Zacchaeus in a fashion something like this: "Our Lord was on His way up to Jerusalem. Great throngs were following Him and they lined the lanes along which He walked. Zacchaeus was a tiny fellow and intensely disliked because he was a tax collector. His business was something of a racket because he was permitted to keep any money he could collect over his quota. He tried to get up in front to see Jesus when He passed by, but the people shouldered him out of the way and shoved him back. Resourcefully, he

101

climbed a tree and crawled out on an overhanging branch, thus affording himself a perfect view.

"When Jesus passed under him He looked up and laughed, saying: 'Zacchaeus, what in the world are you doing up there?' Zacchaeus answered: 'Master, I just wanted to get a good look at you.' With that, our Lord said: 'Come down and join me. I'm going to spend the night at your house.' Poor Zacchaeus almost fell out of the tree in surprised delight. Down he came and on they went together."

The vicar continued in this vein: "Should Jesus come to Pittsburgh today, where do you suppose He would spend the night? Would He go to St. Paul's Roman Catholic Cathedral, seek out the bishop, and ask for a room in his palace? No, I think not. Would he go up to Mt. Lebanon and seek out the Methodist bishop at his manse and ask for a room? No, I think not. Would He go out to Squirrel Hill to the Episcopal bishop's house and request to remain there for the night? No, I think not. Where would He stay?" Then, leaning over the pulpit, the vicar looked at the people in front of him —a downtown congregation made up of all types of people, young, old, rich, poor, married, unmarried—and asked this question:

"Which one of you here this morning is the most despised person in Pittsburgh? Are you or you or you? Well, whoever you are, you are the one Jesus wants to visit. You are the chosen one."

TEACHABILITY AND HUMILITY

CHAPTER NINE

TEACHABILITY AND HUMILITY

The little child is a born inquirer. He is an incurable investigator. He is the original question-asker. He is an inventor and explorer. He creeps and pokes into everything. His eagerness to learn, his open-mindedness, and his teachability will forever be an example for the adult who needs to regain these qualities if he is to obtain a "right judgment in all things."

What happens to us adults who so rapidly digress from all these qualities and proceed to acquire their ugly opposites? As we grow older, we cease to seek the truth if it in any way disturbs our prejudices. What is

107

more, it is not a passive attitude that we develop but one of active antagonism to the truth. Of course, people who read this will rebel against my statement, but do you really not think that what I say is true? It is the rare soul who honestly wants to find out the unattractive facts about himself or about his prejudices—unless he has learned to do so under the guidance of the Holy Spirit.

There is a quality of the Devil himself which seeks to find out the unpleasant information, true or false, about others. According to our Lord, the Church is a place where people congregate to love one another, to have understanding, but never to judge with finality and self-righteousness the conduct of another. He told us that His judgment would be sufficient, that He would give any punishment needed. He also warned that he who judges in a self-righteous sense is in danger of the final judgment. What a ghastly thought for some of us church people! During all of my ministry, I have seen and been a part of groups, (as an unproud participant) who gossip about, judge, and murder characters unmercifully. Woe be unto us! We become self-righteous over our little spiritual practices concerning which, I am sure, our Lord does not care a snap. We church

108

people who belong to the ranks of the unteachable will serve tables, sell trinkets, collect little pledges and piously partake of the Holy Communion. But all of this frenzy does not impress our Lord one single bit if we refuse to seek the truth that makes us free and if we harbor the prejudices that crucify Him.

How can we stay young, attractive, gay and remain supple in mind and body? By becoming as a little child who instinctively wants to know the truth about everything, by taking this native quality and building upon it and applying it to our own attitudes toward ourselves—not morbidly but positively. If we are not willing to make this childlikeness a basic part of our Christian life, it will be far better to stay away from all church relationships. God will be more merciful to the infidel than to that professing Christian who is a saboteur inside the ranks.

Because a little child is teachable, it is easy to lead him to that kind of invaluable humility in which he quickly admits he is wrong and readily repents his misdeeds. If his parents set the example, he will learn to say "I'm sorry" without hesitation. We might add here that this phrase is about the most difficult combination of words for the majority of adults to pronounce. Pride makes it almost impossible for many of us to admit our mistakes or misdeeds. It is this sin which is at the root of endless suffering, divorce, and incalculable disaster.

Igor Sikorsky, one of the greatest airplane designers of our age, told a story of the kind of parental humility which can lead a child to admit his faults and can inspire him to accomplishment. When Sikorsky was a little boy in Kiev, Russia, his father was professor of psychology at the local university. He maintained a small chemical laboratory in his home to which Igor had access. One day, when his father was away at school and his mother was otherwise occupied, the boy busied himself in making a bomb which he pro-ceeded to set off on the front porch. It was far more powerful than he had anticipated, with the result that many of the windows of the house were blown out. The peasant neighbors watched for Papa Sikorsky to come home from the university, and when he came along the lane, they proceeded to recite the news of the explosion. Igor, too, came out to meet his father but his purpose was to make a confession. His father was calm and took the boy into his study, placed him on his knee, and in a kindly way, asked him to tell what hap-

110

pened. Igor stopped crying and told the story, again stating his great penitence for the broken windows. His father assured him that windows could be easily replaced but that few boys could make a successful bomb and congratulated Igor on his experiment. However, he made an agreement with his son that thereafter they would work together on the making of explosives and that neither would set off a detonation without the other being present. Mr. Sikorsky told me that this wonderful example of humility, understanding, and reasonableness on the part of his father taught him the meaning of the mercy of God and greatly stimulated his gift of scientific experimentation. This is borne out by the fact that Mr. Sikorsky produced the first multiple-motored airplane, the first flying boat, and the first successful helicopter (which, in the Korean war and elsewhere, has saved thousands of lives).

When a child is encouraged to admit his mistakes and admits them, it is because fear has been removed from his mind. He knows that if he is open in confessing a wrong action, he will be treated with justice and understanding. Thus, without fear of merciless punishment and abusive outbursts, he is able to be honest with himself and others. He has a chance to succeed in

111

almost any undertaking. Not so, the poor child who cringes in fear because of his mistakes. This misunderstood one finds it necessary to compensate for his terror by learning to cover up. The older he grows, the more false he must build his façade, both with others and himself.

The adults who never admit that they are wrong are legion. We can preach about it and write about it, but they are so conditioned against admitting anything of a negative character that they will not face our words. Instead, they are likely to skip over them or say to themselves that this is exactly the book that somebody else needs. The anaesthetic of self-deception is so strong that they are immunized against all unpleasant truths about themselves. The world finds them out, and wherever they work or live, they eventually find themselves as members of the misfit category. These self-deceivers need help, but no one can do anything for them until such time as they are willing to admit that they are living in a world of false fronts. These people are often possessors of great charm and ability, and yet they go from one disaster to another. Their defences become more acute and clever, and their alibis more complicated and, to the gullible, more convincing.

112

Indeed, the soul who gets caught in this terrorizing whirlpool of self-deception is a prisoner of lies which, in the end, even he begins to believe. All of us are actually more that way than we dare imagine. Are you? Am I? We better find out. Only God's grace, which gives us the ability to see the truth, can make us free from the bondage of lies.

Admission of wrongdoing and mistakes, no matter how frequent is quickly forgiven if it is sincere. We have only to look at the Cross. The good thief turns to Jesus and seeks help, having watched the courageous suffering of the innocent Man. The thief does not dare go as far as to ask for forgiveness but simply says to Him, whom he now recognizes as King through His victory over suffering, "Remember me, Lord, when thou comest into thy kingdom." His only request—to be remembered. That is all Christ needs from the penitent thief—a look, a slight request. As quick as a flash, Jesus answers, "Today shalt thou be with me in Paradise."

And what is so disarming as a little child who comes to you and admits his guilt? What can you do about it other than gather him in your arms and forgive him? Yet, if he runs and hides in fear (because you have made him afraid to tell you the truth), you

113

will chase him and chastise him when you catch him. Instead, if he runs to you in his guilt, you will forgive him and comfort him. Thus, it is easy to teach a little child to repent and confess—but how about you and me?

The old days of one-man, industrial dictatorships are gone. They failed as a result of pride and unteachability. None is more aware of the need of childlike humility today than the intelligent modern industrial leader. Through trial and error, the way of Christ has proved practical. Time and again, I have heard some of the greatest leaders on the American industrial scene say with unquestioning sincerity that humility is a necessity for business success. No man can stay at the top if he is unteachable, stubborn, and domineering. The industrial machine is too complicated and takes many wise heads for its operation. Recently, quite a young man, a leader, in a gigantic business, was developing the fault of stubbornness to such a degree that some of his board told him about it with businesslike directness. At the very next meeting of the Board of Directors, he told the assembly that he was now aware of this weakness and assured them that he was working to eliminate it. His prestige rose immediately. Christianity proves

114

itself to be true, practical, and the only sensible way of life; but we will never know this until we give it a fair trial in practice and action.

A little child is flexible. His body is tough and strong yet supple and elastic. His mind is teachable and, like his body, flexible and elastic. With proper training and example, he can become a wonderful person.

When a man loses his mental, emotional, and spiritual flexibility, he is old. Some are old, stiff, and rigid at heart in their twenties. Others are young, pliable, and resilient in their eighties. Remember that a young spirit tends to perpetuate a youthful body.

And what is more tragic than an old person who is narrow, prejudiced, irritable, unreasonable, and self-righteous—especially if one must live with him and care for him! If you have the courage, you can stand up to a young person who is inflexible and at least battle with him for what is right. But the old person who has become mentally and spiritually petrified is tragic both for himself and for those who must live with him. He is too emotional to listen to reason, too prejudiced to want the truth, and too self-righteous to attend to Godly correction. All one can do is to pray for him, bear with

115

him, and not permit him to rule the household with his devilish tyranny. He may throw childish tantrums of rebellion, but it is far better to have those expressions than to live under the constant poison of appeasement.

More important than thinking about the inflexibility of others, however, is the matter of examining ourselves. Are we going to grow into aged cranks and spread a pall of terrorizing gloom over those we live with, or have relationships with, or are we going to grow old gracefully and thereby remain young eternally. There is a retired actor named Billy Raymond who summers on Long Island, and now is in his eighties. He is a great walker and I pass him frequently. He always has a wonderful smile, a childlike spirit, and an eager hopefulness about him, and, asked his secret, he answered without hesitation, "Austin, if I have the qualities you attribute to me, it is, I suppose because I have always tried to possess a gracious attitude toward all people and toward life in general." Bill is still as flexible and as supple and as elastic in spirit as a child. "Except ye be converted, and become as little children, ye shall not enter into the kingdom of heaven." (*Matt. 18:3*)

If, then, we would desire the wisdom of a right judgment, we will first seek the grace to make it possible. Secondly, we will take our Lord's counsel and study those childlike qualities which are so filled with innate knowledge that we will be led into the truth which shall make us free from the tragedies of unwise decisions and disastrous actions.

TALK IT OUT WITH GOD

CHAPTER TEN

TALK IT OUT WITH GOD

Today most of us have lost a powerful means of communication with God and consequent growth in our association with Him. The phrases of the old gospel hymns, such as "He walks with me and He talks with me," or "Take it to the Lord in prayer," have little practical meaning for most of us. To sing "What a friend we have in Jesus" and to believe in His close companionship are often regarded as mere sentimentalities by the intellectuals and rationalists of religion. By adhering to outward ecclesiastical formalism, we have become inwardly "tied up." We have lost much of the sense of free communion with the Holy Spirit.

121

Someone facetiously called Episcopalians "God's frozen people." For some of us, he was not too far from the truth. We are often either too self-conscious to be natural with God or too lacking in the virtue of childlike simplicity to be able to have a sense of free communion with a Father who desires to be intimate with us. Our false sense of propriety causes us to argue that we fear fanaticism. Yet, we see little, if any, evidence of such a danger in present-day Protestantism—especially as practiced by the respectable orthodox.

A sense of the immediate presence of God is the first belief that must be made real if we are to converse on friendly terms with the Divine Presence. Some modern interpreters have tended to change the meaning of the Biblical phrase, "the Kingdom of God is within you," to say it merely means "among you." The Christian religion, however, is charged with the concept of the indwelling of God. This has held true throughout all manifestations of the religion for many generations.

St. Paul says, "He is above all, through all, and in you all." Again, we are told in John's Gospel that within each of us is the "Light, which lighteth every man that cometh into the world." Great phrases of the liturgy make continued reference to this inward relationship that exists through the indwelling presence of God. At confirmation, we pray that we "may daily increase in thy Holy Spirit more and more." This is said as one receives the Divine Gift at the laying on of hands. In the Holy Communion, we pray "that He may evermore dwell in us and we in Him." When we receive the sacrament inwardly in our lives, the prayer of outward reception is said by the administrator as follows: "The Body of our Lord Jesus Christ, which was given for thee, preserve thy body and soul unto everlasting life. Take and eat this in remembrance that Christ died for thee, and feed on him in thy heart by faith, with thanksgiving." There can be no doubt that the Christian religion presupposes that God is within us, above us, beneath us, about us, and closer to us than we are to ourselves. Thus, He is always ready to communicate with us.

The Bible and the saints of history give constant testimony to the fact that those who have been close to God were ever ready to debate with Him, wrestle with Him, praise Him, chide Him, and plead with Him concerning their problems. They felt no compunction about asking help and counsel from Him on any occasion and for any personal or social need. God walked

123

and talked with them, and they were respectful, but direct and open with Him, in all areas of their lives. Many of the great saints talked to Him with such un-self-conscious naturalness that the charm of their conversations is delightfully poetic. But rarely, if ever, does it occur to us that we too can have communications of equal naturalness and simplicity if we will only permit ourselves to become less self-conscious.

A story is told of the great St. Theresa of Avila concerning a journey she once made with a band of fifty nuns. As they were on their way to the convent, she led them across a shaky bridge in the midst of a tremendous storm. The waters of the small stream were turbulent, and the nuns prayed continuously that the bridge would not wash out before they got across. When they were in the middle of the bridge, however, it collapsed, and the holy women were all plunged into the river. They fished one another out successfully and stood shivering on the bank. St. Theresa lifted her eyes to the heavens and reproached God saying, "If this is the way You treat Your friends, it is no wonder that You have so many enemies."

The admonition of the Bible that tells us to go into our closets in secret and close the door and there talk openly with God may be taken literally. We humbly accept the technique of consultation in a psychiatrist's office where, behind closed doors, we stretch ourselves out on a couch and talk freely about our emotions, ideas, and actions while the doctor tabulates the information on his pad. Psychiatry, in the right hands, can be of invaluable help, but there is no good reason why we should not let the God within us be our psychiatrist. Talk freely and out loud to Him about your problems and do so at length until you have divulged your real feelings in His presence. If you are honest with Him and with yourself, you will begin to get both the right answers and a vision of how to take your next step.

There is much value in talking aloud to God. Of course, it may be wise to let the family know what you are doing lest they be tempted to send for the man in the white coat. Nevertheless, if they understand what you are up to, you can begin to have a sense of freedom that will soon develop into a deep and practical spiritual experience. The value of audible conversation is a real one because you, yourself, hear what you say; and it is less easy to fool yourself when your words are spoken aloud before God. Likewise, the very fact that you hear what you say makes a much deeper impression if you

125

have arrived at the point where you can begin to forget yourself. Self-forgetfulness comes with practice and prayer.

The monastic tradition has always emphasized a rule that priests repeat their offices aloud if possible. Otherwise, they should do so with at least a physical movement of the lips. One is much less apt to daydream during prayer if the act of praying is physically expelled from the lips, even though it be an inaudible whisper.

What was said in the preceding chapter is important in this connection. If we are to talk freely, it must be done with as much truth and grace as we possess. Frequently, in my own experience, for instance, I have paced the floor during a sleepless night when bothered by a problem. Out loud, I have talked over my problem with God. Then, I have allowed the highest knowledge within me to answer audibly. When I prayed that the truth be spoken, I never found that I fooled myself. Eventually, the wise answer came.

Talking aloud with God cannot be struck up in a frantic moment of despair and indecision. We must have some background and practice in the skill of carrying on a conversation with the Almighty. We do not become expert conversationalists by being silent and not talking.

We should begin by thinking of conversations with God as we go through the day and, if possible, we should move our lips enough to make the discussion more real. It is of the utmost importance that we be realistic and direct with God when we have such discussions. If we do not feel like praying, we should say so. If there are questions that confront us which we do not care to face, it is wise to tell God exactly how we feel. Our Lord Himself set the example in the Garden of Gethsemane when He told His Father that He did not want to drink of the cup that was about to be presented. On the Cross, He spoke with utmost candor when He questioned the Father, saying: "My God, my God, why hast thou forsaken me?" If we feel depressed, dissatisfied with our lot, or unwilling to do that which we ought to do, it is sensible to be honest. He knows our real thoughts anyway, and we are in a much more healthy frame of mind if we openly express them.

This habit, requires practice in the little doings throughout the day. Slowly and surely, we can develop a feeling of intimacy with God who dwells in the heart

127

of every man, for within us is His indwelling Presence. Honesty with God and ourself in conversation will lead directly toward the answer that will guarantee "a right judgment in all things." Then we will be on our way toward unity with God's universal laws as well as to certain victory in every undertaking.

WISE AS A SERPENT

CHAPTER ELEVEN

WISE AS A SERPENT

One of the greatest opportunities to see the importance of right judgment is to observe its use in relation to the truth. Jesus said, "I am the truth." We Christians, therefore cannot be loyal to a life of prayer and sacrament if we do not develop opportunities to express Christlike judgments at the expense of our selfish and personal inclinations. Right judgments do not spring from a self-centered habit of doing and saying whatever is the simplest and easiest, at the time, for ourselves.

Let us take this problem, for example: Are there times when we should withhold the truth? This should not be misunderstood as the question: Should we ever

131

tell a lie? Our question is more subtle. Are there times, we are asking, in which the easiest and selfish course is to spill everything (true as what we say may be), when the harder, but more loving course, is to remain silent? It would seem that Jesus often has in mind these latter situations.

Of course, we should always be truthful and upright. But the obligation to develop right judgment does not mean that we must become blundering bulls who blurt out all that we must think and know at any impulsive moment. Our Lord Himself tells us that not all people are ready for all the facts at every stage of their development. "Cast not your pearls before swine," is the rather forceful way it is put in Matthew.

In the Gospels, Jesus implies in numerous instances that He is withholding many of His great perceptions. He withholds His insights from time to time because His people are not ready to receive them. He even has to give them the full truth in stories and parables.

Rather than this being a question of dishonesty, this is a valid lesson. It teaches us that in each situation a right judgment is required to decide what is or is not appropriate. In our everyday life we can see opportunities for the application of this wisdom.

132

Some people are not entitled to know the truth. Should everyone know the entire truth about nuclear fission? Some would be overwhelmed by it and not know what to do with the momentous secret. Others could not be trusted not to use it to harm themselves and their neighbor. A right judgment in situations in which we are not obligated to tell all we know—at least, not all at once—requires that we be as gentle as a dove, yet as wise as a serpent. Many times weak and sensitive people can be seriously maimed by the naked truth, and for their sakes we protect them by silence or by meeting them where they are with the diet of truth they can digest. The truth, like medicine, will cure. But a wise doctor does not judge that the same quantity is good for everyone—nor does he always give all that he has at one sitting.

Now let us turn to ourselves. Many of us can not possibly accept the entire truth about ourselves all at once. If our varied weaknesses, our subconscious repressions, our mixed-up motives, and our selfish impulses were laid bare—as if at Judgment Day—we could not face them. God, in His infinite provision for us, has understood this and so has designed another method. As we seek the truth, He will reveal it, but

133

in degrees that will not overwhelm us. Then, He will continually forgive us so that we will not be overcome by a shriveling sense of guilt. Offensive to Him as is our selfishness and our carelessness, His mercy and loving-kindness can transcend them. His nature is to forgive, and thus we need never be overwhelmed with a deadening burden of guilt. Thus, He allows us to find out our weaknesses as we go along, and He helps us meet them in such a way that they do not frustrate us.

Does God withhold the truth from those who seek after a right judgment? In one sense, as we can see, even He, because He understands us, does. He does not reveal the whole truth about our sinful self to us at one shattering instance. Thanks to His mercy, He lets us discover the truth in the degree that we can accept. To some, it will be more gradual than to others. For all, however, He has the same plan and purpose. He does not want to force us into a life of guilty depression. Instead, He wants us to live a sacrificial life of positive advance and joyous victory.

There are times when a right judgment says that the truth must be forthrightly told and not withheld.

When people are harmful to their neighbors and to themselves, the truth must be told. It is a sin to tolerate the destructiveness of lies and selfishness. Politeness, sentimentality, and fear lest a tyrant break out in an outburst must be cast aside. In their place must come a Christian presentation of the facts.

Recently, I was told of a church school superintendent who was damaging the nurture of the children in his parish. The teachers disliked him and the youngsters feared him. As a matter of fact, it would have been better had the church school been discontinued. It brewed gossip, animosity, and general unpleasantness. The rector, however, was afraid to face the tyrant. He feared an explosion.

In the parish, there were a few courageous mothers. They decided to make the rector face the truth about the tyrant; and in no uncertain terms, they stated that they would withdraw their children and send them to some other church school if something were not done. This forced the rector to pray and to reconsider the entire matter. The result was a more correct judgment.

There was indeed a terrible explosion, with a certain minority group joining in with the selfish superintendent. The mothers, however, were right, and the misguided personality was relieved of his post. Several parishioners left the church, but today this particular school prospers and has doubled in its spirituality as well as in its attendance. A new attitude of Christian charity and joy permeates the fellowship. Thus, we can see that a compromise with destructiveness by omitting to face the truth is, in certain cases, as detrimental to right judgment as a too great willingness to tell the truth (when the circumstances are not appropriate) is in other cases. A fear to face the truth in situations that rightly call for courageous action is a great stumbling block in the path of right judgment.

There is the kind of quasi-Christian leader who has a passion to rule his kingdom (be his parish or group little or small) by dominating others through giving them an unabsolved sense of guilt when they do not do what he says must be done. These subjects become cold and inwardly resentful. Yet, in their ignorance of the true spirit of Christianity, they are afraid to speak out. They rationalize that their fear of the power-practitioner is what the Sermon on the Mount means by *meekness*, and in their mistaken judgment about the nature of Christian humility, they permit an evil condition, within their power to cure, to go on.

It is appalling how many Christian institutions are dominated by some little ecclesiastical Hitler who mouths religious phrases and at the same time, by his very acts and attitudes, denies the first premise of Christian charity. True Christianity rests on a spirit of unity and fellowship among people who come to an agreement through the guidance of the Holy Spirit. They show a mutual willingness to surrender their wills to God's wisdom. But the leader who dominates others —no matter how pious he may profess to be—is neither a teacher of Christianity nor a minister of the Gospel of love and forgiveness. Furthermore, no Christian fellowship exists in his parish—especially if the members of the group are afraid to constructively criticize or disagree with his tyrannical tactics—in the spirit, of course, of unprejudiced love. No. The spirit of true Christianity can never exist in a parish or in a society until there is unity and fellowship among people who come to an agreement through the guidance of the Holy Spirit.

Before one starts telling people the truth (as he sees it), one should be sure that the idea being entertained is really true. This implies that we first get the facts straight. If this is done, and we know them with accuracy, we may pray that our judgments—if we must make them—may be made clear, concise, and correct. Emotional, "straight from the shoulder" talk without the preparation of facts and prayer is too often self-righteous, egotistical, and incorrect. Those who are always bragging that they call "a spade a spade" in the name of religion are likely to do more harm to the faith than good. These people tend to speak out in the name of the Lord, but what they say is both unfair to Him and damaging to His Church.

When you are faced with the necessity of talking directly to a person who needs to reckon with the truth, you should take time to ask God to prepare the way and to arrange a timely opening. Furthermore, it is wise to ask for the gift to follow through and do your duty without procrastination. Furthermore, you should also pray for the grace to be patient enough to refrain from advice until it seems right to talk. In other words, except in immediate emergencies, the speaking of the truth to one another needs spiritual preparation.

In speaking the unsolicited, or even solicited truth, to others the first task is the prayer that you may christianly love the person to whom the truth is to be told. If you speak with a trace of anger, resentment, or self-righteousness, you will defeat your purpose. Your very attitude of antagonism will telegraph an atmosphere which in all probability will cause the other person to reject what you have judged it right to say.

Right judgment is an all-important part of the manifestation of prayer and sacrament. Thus, a Christian must seek God's grace first before he can have a judgment that will be right, for if the decisions he makes do not stem from worship, they are vain and not redeemed by God's love.

"THUS SAITH THE LORD"

CHAPTER TWELVE

"THUS SAITH THE LORD"

Negative thought patterns prevent us from making right judgments. The intriguing phrase, "Thus saith the Lord," points to a technique that can be most effective in freeing us from inner attitudes that have made us captive personalities of destructive thought.

In a sense each one of us has two natures. We have a lower man, a material man, an old Adam type of man, a selfish man making up our human nature on the one hand. On the other, we have the potentiality for a higher man, a spiritual man, a redeemed man, a man with the indwelling Spirit of Christ as a part of our

143

nature. These two men within each of us continually battle for supremacy. We seek the "grace and consolation of the Holy Spirit" so that the higher man may win the day and attain the victory. It is the higher man that must dominate the lower man and keep him in line; and this is reasonably possible.

In the Prayer Book the ministration of Holy Baptism points out this duality of human personality. At the outset we are told "None can enter into the kingdom of God, except he be regenerate and born anew of Water and the Holy Ghost." Again, we pray that "this Child may enjoy the everlasting benediction of thy heavenly washing, and may come to the eternal kingdom . . ."

Further reference to this dual nature of man is emphasized at baptism when we say, "We have prayed that our Lord Jesus Christ would vouchsafe to receive you, *to release you from sin,* to sanctify you with the Holy Ghost, to give you the kingdom of heaven, and everlasting life." (*P.B.,* p. 277. Italics mine.) Then the sponsors are prepared for the renunciation of "the devil and all his works, the vain pomp and glory of the world, with all covetous desires of the same, *and the sinful*

144

desires of the flesh, so that thou [they] wilt not follow,
nor be led by them." (*P.B.*, p. 277. Italics mine.)

Further on, such prayers as these are stated:

Grant that all sinful affections may die in him, and that
all things belonging to the Spirit may live and grow in
him. *Amen.*

Grant that he may have power and strength to have
victory, and to triumph, against the devil, the world, and
the flesh. *Amen.* (*P.B.*, p. 278.)

St. Paul says, "Put off the old man and put on the
new man which is Christ." He further gave us a clue to
victory when he said, "I live, yet not I but Christ liveth
within me."

Since each one of us has two natures, that of the
earth and that which is spiritual, it is reasonable and
sensible to pray to God for grace and strength and
sacramental power to talk convincingly to that lower
nature which dominates our thoughts and actions so
much of the time. This, in other words, is to practice
the habit of allowing God in our higher selves to speak
to the Adam in our lesser selves so that the lower man
may be brought into line and kept in his place. Thus,
the two natures work constructively together.

145

Psychiatrists are aware of the destructive drainage of energy that comes from the disintegration of personality. This is the result of the split in one's character that makes us halt between two opinions. I read of a turtle that was found in Florida and taken to the zoology department of a university. The reptile had one shell, four legs, and two heads. It had lived happily with itself in its home water, but when taken out it began to waste away. The two heads had different ideas as to the direction the body should take when hunting food, and a nervous breakdown seemed to engulf the turtle. It was then put back into the pond where again it lived happily with itself. In the water one head looked below the surface for food while the other remained above to take in air. I do not know how accurate this newspaper account is, but certainly the dual natures in most of us keep us in a state of constant indecision and near-nervous collapse. Peace within comes from the domination of the lower nature by the higher nature. Then cooperation, health, and good living proceed automatically.

A fact that we must all become more aware of is that we talk to ourselves most of the time whether we know what we are saying or not. It all depends upon

146

who is talking to whom. If a person is not spiritually alert, his lower nature will dominate the conversation, continually giving suggestions to the total personality. Such thoughts are dominated by fleshly desire, selfish motivation, jealousy, fear, resentment, hatred, anger, inferiority, self-pity, a power complex, and avarice.

Watch the average person on any busy corner as he passes into the revolving doors of a store. Note the expression of fatigue, distress, and general unhappiness. As a matter of fact, look upon ourselves at almost any time when we are not concentrating on some definite task, and we will see that the thoughts that we have allowed to dominate us have generally taken hold and established permanent negative attitudes that tend toward our total defeat. Thus, it is of practical value consciously to establish a habit of talking from the higher self, with the aid of God and His means of grace, to the lower self. Since we are talking to ourselves unwittingly most of the time, we ought to establish a consciously constructive pattern for this inward conversation.

It is true that we are often influenced by the thoughts of others, but it is what we tell ourselves that has the most important effect. It is well to keep a note-

147

book and record the kinds of thoughts you are telling yourself many hours of the day. You can catch up with yourself during your conscious moments by jotting down the number of negative, fretful, and sinful attitudes that dominate your thinking. You will then begin to realize how devastating the power of destructive suggestion is. The only way out is to ask God's help through a prayer such as "cleanse the thoughts of our hearts by the inspiration of Thy Holy Spirit," and then plan a positive program.

A positive conversation with your lower self emanating from God in the reborn man can go like this: "John, you are a child of God and an inheritor of the Kingdom of Heaven. That is what your faith teaches, and it is the truth. You need fear no man since you have confessed your sins to God, and you have received His forgiveness and power. Therefore, John, all you need to do is to believe that there is no room for inferiority, no room for fear, no room for resentment.

"John, my friend, God is with you, above you, through you, beneath you, and about you. God is your close friend—He is closer to you than you are to yourself. He never fails. All you need to do is believe, believe, believe, believe! Remember this a thousand times

148

a day, for His power and grace are equal to every problem and every need.

"John, above everything else, watch out for self-pity. It will destroy you and weaken you and make you vulnerable to any and every kind of attack from the forces of evil. You must watch that one like a hawk, for it creeps in in the most devastating and unsuspecting manner. Call upon God at all hours to bring all His forces of destruction down upon this devil of self-pity. Self-pity means that you are so in love with yourself that there is no room for the love of God. You take everything, therefore, that everyone says in the wrong way. You look at all events as if you were the center of the universe, and you slowly but surely destroy your own usefulness. You become helpless.

"John, keep your chin up and join with me in thinking unselfishly, serving man, and fearing nothing. God is with us and together we can do all things. Remember that our Lord said, 'If two of you shall agree on earth as touching any thing that they shall ask, it shall be done for them of my Father.' Let's continue to pray this together, John, and work as a team. Then we shall have the power that God intended us to possess and express."

This is merely a crude suggestion of the kind of

149

conversation a person can build up within himself as a form of prayer. It can go on day in and day out and re-place the unconscious, negative conversations that de-stroy us and leave God almost entirely out of the picture.

COURAGE FOR ACTION

CHAPTER THIRTEEN

COURAGE FOR ACTION

Christianity is a personal adventure in making decisions and taking action. There are occasions when we need counsel and guidance from wise people, but generally speaking, it is possible to come to strong conclusions alone with God. When in serious doubt, we must have the humility to consult a trusted spiritual friend, but ordinarily a Christian is stronger if he stands on his own two feet with God. If we want the truth, God has given us the basic inner equipment to know it. This inner knowledge, as we have said before, is not dependent upon formal education or even upon informa-

153

tion about the technicalities of religion and of the Bible, but rather upon the inner integrity of motive united with the righteous laws that are behind the operation of the universe.

Right judgment does not require that we be morally perfect. No man is without sin. If it were necessary for us to wait for right decisions until such time as we achieved moral and spiritual perfection, we would spend our lives as the victims of chaotic calculations and disastrous actions. What is required is a desire for God's truth, wanted so badly that we will sacrifice obstacles that stand in the way; not all at once, but one at a time. Have you ever known a person who wanted the truth as guidance for future action who could not obtain it if he was an honest seeker after the will of God. He will slip and fail, as do most Christian travelers, but if he chooses to follow Jesus as his over-all guide, he will inevitably be led to the truth.

When the strong inward sense that tells us what ought to be done arrives, it is then necessary to have the grace, the spiritual strength and courage, for action. Sometimes that action must be drastic in its effect upon human relationships. It may break up friendships. Sometimes it involves loss of finances and personal pleasure.

Nevertheless, it must be approached with the confidence and courage of a surgeon who sees that only a major operation can possibly save the patient. He realizes that it is better to operate in the hope of saving a life than to hesitate, knowing that death probably will be inevitable.

On such occasions, the immediate members of the family are rarely in a position to make clear-cut decisions about one another. They are too close to the scene. A man of my acquaintance endured a severe spinal operation, and it was necessary to stop the surgery before the doctor completed his work. Death was hovering over the table. A few weeks later, the patient recovered sufficiently to undergo another operation. This time it might mean death, but without an operation it would mean constant pain and a crippling existence, as well as suffering and tragedy for all concerned. Having heard the counsel of wise surgeons, the family was advised to go ahead with the venture and take the risk. His wife, naturally, was in no condition to decide alone. She agreed, and the delicate spinal surgery was completed with great skill and courage. The patient lived and improved vastly.

There are occasions when we may need outside

counsel, as I have said, and others when we need the courage of a lion to attack a situation and, with Paul, "having done all, stand."

In small but crucial ways, my mother showed Christian spiritual courage. When I was about fifteen years of age, I was working in a drugstore at night and made a habit of going out with a neighborhood gang after work every evening about ten o'clock. As a rule I was home before midnight, but for a fifteen-year-old boy it was too late according to her standards.

One evening, she told me that I must return home immediately after work. I agreed casually; and when work ended, I proceeded to hang around a Chicago street corner as usual. When I arrived home, my mother was waiting up with righteous anger. She told me to pack my clothes and leave. I was stunned. She told me that the time apparently had come when I was making the rules of conduct for our modest five-room flat, and therefore I had to live elsewhere. She explained that she was still the ruler of the household and would continue to be in all matters of my discipline until I came of age. At that time I could make my own rules. Until then, as long as I had taken the authority into my own hands, I could live elsewhere. She meant every word she said, so I left the house to roam the streets for what seemed hours to me.

Finally, filled with remorse, I returned home like the prodigal son and begged to be admitted. I promised that thereafter I would obey the rules of the house which were fair and just. My mother found it necessary to cut deeply into my character with the scalpel of courage and righteous judgment. It paid dividends for me as well as for her.

Once again, she found that I had written excuses for high school absences and had played hooky with regularity. To her this was forgery, although it was not quite so serious to my high school pals and myself. She marched me down to the office of the principal, Mr. Bogen, of Chicago's Lane Technical High School. She produced the letters of excuse I had written and told the principal that now she was unable to trust me. She asked to be notified thereafter of all absences. It was a humiliating but a courageous stand on her part, and I learned something about the meaning of old-fashioned biblical character and integrity.

When one has sought and found the spiritual courage to take strong stands in the face of enormous risks, one receives dividends from God that are almost be-

157

yond measure. In the long run, God never lets a person down who makes righteous judgments of great courage, if the judgments have no egocentric air of self-righteousness about them. It is always wise to add this warning: Beware lest you think that you are infinitely more righteous than others when you make such decisions. You must have the confidence that God has shown you the truth but that you yourself are still filled with human frailty and, while asking for His mercy on your own behalf, proceed with such light as you may have to follow through, awaiting whatever may come in the name of Christ.

When decisions are made and placed in action, one begins to feel a new sense of freedom and security. One then knows the meaning of the phrase of the Book of Common Prayer, "whose service is perfect freedom." You are no longer tied and shackled by the paralysis of fear that comes over you when the truth is seen but only cowardice prevails. Freedom of action is a great spiritual experience because you have prayed enough to believe that the truth will make you free and that actions will result in final victory and benefit for all concerned. Furthermore, you know that the penalty for not having followed through with such decisions will mean some form of disaster for you and also for everyone else concerned with you.

Some years ago I attended the Episcopal Church's General Convention in Kansas City. Early one morning on my way to Holy Communion, I met Frances Perkins, then Secretary of Labor. We walked many blocks to the church and knelt together for the opening of the service. She reached into her huge purse and pulled out a well-worn and thoroughly thumbed book of devotions and proceeded to lose herself deeply in her prayers. I was greatly impressed.

At the end of the service we walked back to the hotel, and I asked her how she was able to be so strong and well in the midst of the many crises she faced daily. (At that time, Frances Perkins was being lampooned by every cartoonist in the country, and unjust things were said of her.) She smiled and said that she went to Holy Communion almost every day and there offered her life and her work and her decisions to Almighty God. She added that there was no question but that she made unwise decisions at times, yet they were the best she could offer God under the conditions. She proceeded to tell me that the wonderful part of God's mercy was that under such conditions she always found

159

that God balanced off the wrong decisions with added grace in other departments and in the long run her life and work turned out successfully. The fear that haunted her more than anything else, she said, was the inability to make decisions in faith and to act on the assumption that it was the best she knew in the sight of God at the particular moment. She repeated that when she was wrong, God always seemed to help her out of the difficulty. What is more, she did not know the meaning of insomnia.

Spiritual courage for a Christian is not, of course, acquired in a moment, any more than Frances Perkins acquired it in a moment; but the more you think about it and pray about it and seek it, the more you will become a person of enormous will power, and your accomplishments (in whatever station in life you find yourself) will become prodigious. Your neighbors may not always like you, but they will never have any attitude toward you other than that of respect. They may gossip about you, but in the final analysis, when they themselves are in trouble, they will turn to you because they know that you possess the qualities of truth and courage which will strengthen them and make them free.

160

When you pray for the grace of courage and then take action, there is no question but that you will make occasional mistakes. Sometimes these mistakes will be costly. Nevertheless, these mistakes are preferable to a "halt between two opinions" and thus being neither right nor wrong, but sick and frustrated.

Christianity is a personal adventure in making decisions and taking action. God always makes up the deficit in wrong decisions.

BEWARE OF APPROVAL AND APPEASEMENT

CHAPTER FOURTEEN

BEWARE OF APPROVAL
AND APPEASEMENT

The world is full of worthy and sweet people who lack courage and thus are continually bearing burdens that ought to be shared by others. They live the lives of drones. Drone-life is all right for bees, but there is no evidence that God ever intended it for human beings. In most cases, the human drones lose their "sting" because they lack the courage to demand that others bear their share of burdens when they are capable of doing so. For some reason they think that there is virtue in lifting a load for someone who is perfectly able to lift it for himself.

Burden-bearers are always trying to smooth over the rough places that are made intolerable by tyrants and cry-babies. More often than not, the burden-bearer is the mother of a large brood. She is likely to carry the burden for the whole family and nobly bear up when she ought to bear down. By appeasing, she tries to keep everyone at peace.

Selfish tyrants or loafers may be in the immediate family, either a parent, a grandparent, a husband, a wife, a child, a brother, a sister, or some other relative. The family burden-bearer continually follows the policy of appeasement toward these people; and when she does so, she cannot help but lessen her own self-respect. She must compromise issues and in so doing knows that she is shielding others from facing the truth with justice.

The burden-bearer lives under bullying tactics or self-pitying pressure and continues, beyond all reason, to bear the brunt of everyone's trouble. This person will usually grow more and more resentful within her subconscious and, eventually, illness will overtake her. She cannot stand up under the conflicts that go on inside, for deep in her heart she knows she is being weak and giving in to the selfishness of others. Furthermore,

166

the appeaser is contributing to the sins of the tyrant and the loafer, and is only making him worse by condoning his delinquency.

The doctrine of peace at any price never pays, and the longer it is sustained, the more disastrous is the cataclysmic result. The appeaser will become broken and ill, and the bully will go from one destructive experience to another.

There are times, of course, when one cannot help falling into situations that call for temporary appeasement. Sometimes, especially if we live under circumstances that make us, or those near us, economically dependent upon bullies, we are forced into positions of weakness. Then the greater good may demand that we suffer the humiliation. In such cases, however, we ought to have the constant counsel of strong Christian leadership.

In this chapter, we are not thinking about rare situations, but about the burden-bearers of countless thousands of families and businesses throughout the nation. In these cases, we will be far better off if, on the whole, we stand for the truth and for what is unselfish in ourselves and in others with whom we must live. It is amazing how those who abuse other people

167

will knuckle under when they find that we really mean business and will stand up to our convictions.

A clergyman with ability was called to be a rector of a large parish when he was in his late twenties. Unconsciously he tended to be a sadist. He made his wife suffer by continually dwelling on the difficulty of his work. When she suggested answers to the daily problems that he brought home, he invariably frustrated her by proving there were no answers to his difficulties. He insisted that what he should do was to get away from his impossible parish and take a small country church. For several weeks, he harped on the simple country life as being a paradise compared to the terrible burdens in his large parish.

One night the rector came home to find his courageous wife had come to the realization that he needed an ultimatum. She saw clearly that she was indulging him through her overdrawn patience and understanding. He started in on his nightly wail. She stopped him and said, "I married you for better or for worse and I will go anywhere in the Church you so desire. I will stay here in this fine big parish, or I will go into the country. But, I refuse to stay here and be your wife and listen to these frustrating tirades night after

168

night. Either stay here and do your job and keep quiet
or go to the country and keep quiet. Make up your
mind, and I mean it."

This woman had ceased to bear her husband's emotional burdens and had borne down on his character.
He knew that she meant it. He stopped feeling sorry
for himself, stayed, and became one of the outstanding
clergymen in the long history of the parish.

The burden-bearer who reads this may recognize
himself as an habitual appeaser. Remember, however,
that patience and understanding must generally come
before decisive action. A sudden desire to be free must
not make us act impulsively (of this, more later). We
must realize that appeasement is not as harmful in its
relationship to ourselves as it is to the people we allow
to live with their habit of abuse to others. If we encourage others to live a life of selfish injustice toward us,
we are guilty of making them into gross monsters, and
the semblance virtue of kindliness we practice toward
them is no virtue at all but a fearsome vice. Then too,
realize that the other person, the tryrant or the loafer,
is being harmed the most.

We caution you against reading this and thinking
suddenly that it fits you and therefore (in your anger)

169

that you should demand your rights or should launch an outbreak of righteous indignation. Generally, we start bravely on such a venture but soon weaken and fade back into a worse position than that which we occupied at the outset. We do not have the inner strength or the sustaining grace to carry through with our impetuous start; neither have we brought God sufficiently into the picture to have wisdom to make the transition either for ourselves or for any others concerned. It is far better to begin to pray about it with consistency and to attend Holy Communion regularly, offering special intentions at the altar: for the other person's weaknesses; for the strengthening of our own characters; and for further light on the situation so that it may be handled with Christian wisdom, character, love, and justice.

You may have to pray out a situation of this kind for weeks or even months; but by staying at it, by seeking the courage that God alone can give, He will begin to change the character, not only of yourself, but of the other person or persons concerned. Opportunities eventually will arise whereby the strength of Christ will begin to shine through you, and you will not react with inner anger, resentment, and depression but rather with patience, strength, and a firm hope. You will no longer appease with a false and frozen smile, but you will begin to take on the firm countenance of a Christian character whose inward force will change outward environment.

There are many reasons why some people become human drones and live by being the appeasers for everybody. One of the main causes is the desire to seek approval. We like to be loved, to be approved, and to become popular. Therefore, we tend never to object to the standards of anyone unless they be of a station that is inferior to our own. We will often take strong stands when we believe that we are dealing with people who are "beneath us." With our so-called equals and superiors, we continue to be agreeable, attractive, smiling, and at all times uncontroversial.

This matter of approval is a widespread and common problem. It becomes so partly because it is natural for us to want to be liked, and partly because it is right that we should want to be liked. For most of us, it is important that we have the good opinion and approbation of our fellow beings. Although it may be hard to make clear, there is a fine line between a normal man's social desire to be liked, respected, and even admired

171

and the inner compulsion to tailor our behavior and words to what will please others. This whole matter, however, is a complex psychological phenomenon and crops up in many different guises.

The problem of approval is unbelievably general. Let us realize this now. It is the rare person who does not suffer from it to some degree, and it requires a good deal of prayer if he is to be made whole.

When we live the life of approval-seeking inferiority, we become more and more disgusted with ourselves and resentful about all others concerned. Yet we dare not show it, and therefore we become victims of insomnia, stomach ulcers, neuritis, arthritis, and every imaginable kind of ailment that can result from the fact that we have committed internal perjury. It upsets our inward emotional systems and causes the mismanagement of our glandular secretions and sets up added muscular tensions. Illness of one kind or another inevitably follows.

Why do we seek the approval of others? Dr. Grosvenor Pearson, a Pittsburgh psychiatrist, gives a simple answer. It is because we have not yet approved our own judgment of ourselves. Thus, we do not believe that the Kingdom of God is within us and that, having prayed and sought for the truth, we can arrive at right judgments and stand by them. Once we have failed to believe in our own judgment, we tend to lead a life of approval-seeking because, as he says, we have not approved of ourselves. Thus, we become slaves of public opinion, and we are inwardly shaken to bits by conflicting emotions and confused motives. If we do not seek the companionship of God and the acceptance of ourselves that comes from knowing that we have done our best through Him, then we must continually look for others to pat us on the back and tell us that we are wonderful. If we cannot obtain that from them, we seek it by agreeing with and toadying to their bullying and unjust tactics. Thus, the secret of the problem of finding-approval-from-the-outside is first to obtain the approval of ourselves on the inside. This approval comes from learning to stand alone in prayer with Almighty God and as Paul says, "having done all, stand."

Here is the place where we should remind ourselves again that there is a spot in life for the right kind of self-love. It must be in accord with Christ's command to love our neighbors as ourselves. This command, of course, also means that we are to love ourselves as we love our neighbors. Somewhere along the

173

line there has developed an attitude toward *loving one's self* that has been altogether destructive. Thus, self-approval through prayerful conference with Christ has become a lost art. That is why we seek the approval of men rather than the approval of God. Once we have descended to this standard, we cannot love ourselves, and therefore we can love no one else. This is a subtle sin that can be cured by seeking "a right judgment in all things" through continued communion with Christ in prayer and the Holy Sacraments.

The Epistle for the third Sunday in Advent, taken from Chapter 4 of I Corinthians, states the call to despise man's judgment and to exalt God's. "But with me it is a very small thing that I should be judged of you, or of man's judgment: yea, I judge not mine own self. For I know nothing against myself; yet am I not hereby justified: but he that judgeth me is the Lord. Therefore judge nothing before the time, until the Lord come, who both will bring to light the hidden things of darkness, and will make manifest the counsels of the hearts . . ."

Again, in the Epistle to the Romans, St. Paul says: "Owe no man anything, but to love one another." (*Rom.* 13:8.)

In Chapter 22 of Matthew, a similar note is emphasized when the Pharisees took counsel how they
might entangle Him by much talk, saying: "Master, we
know that thou art true, and teachest the way of God
in truth, neither carest thou for any man: for thou re-
gardest not the person of men." Here again, even as
they tried to entangle Him, they were forced to admit
that He feared no human opinion whatsoever.

In the book of Proverbs, we see a statement that
may fit all of those who fear the call to listen only to
the voice of God rather than to that of worldly opinions: "Because I have called and ye refused—I will also
laugh at your calamity. I will mock when your fear cometh as a whirlwind, when distress and anguish cometh
upon you."

Nothing can bring more anguish and calamity upon
us than the habit of continual appeasement of men
who, we know, are not sharing their burdens or are not
standing for what we know is true. To the degree we
appease and compromise, we shall "reap the whirlwind"
of inner conflict and outward disaster.

Again, we quote Paul: "My brethren, be strong in
the Lord, and in the power of his might. Put on the
whole armour of God, that ye may be able to stand

175

against the wiles of the devil. For we wrestle not against flesh and blood, but against principalities, against powers, against rulers of the darkness of this world, against spiritual wickedness in high places. Wherefore take unto you the whole armour of God, that ye may be able to withstand in the evil day, and having done all, to stand." (*Eph.* 6:10-13.)

The problem of approval is, as we have discovered, complex. Its solution, however, can never depend on unreasonable burden-bearing or appeasement, nor can it depend on disapproval of self. Burden-bearing and appeasement are rooted in a mistaken understanding of kindness and are harmful to others, while the lack of proper self-love—the self-love that comes through prayerful conference with Christ—is harmful not only to one's physical and emotional life, but also to one's ability to possess a true and divinely given "right judgment in all things."

GOOD AND BAD JUDGMENT IN EVANGELISM

CHAPTER FIFTEEN

GOOD AND BAD JUDGMENT IN EVANGELISM

There is an encouraging trend in the Christian Church which expresses itself in group movement. Evangelistic healing, study, and prayer groups are springing up in various churches throughout America by the hundreds. They are deepening faith, strengthening religion, and carrying into practical application many emphases of the Gospel which have been unexpressed during our generation.

The group movement is proving itself an asset with vast possibilities for the rebuilding of a vital and personalized Christianity for our time. In many aspects it is one of the most hopeful religious developments today

179

and, interestingly enough, instead of coming from denominational headquarters, it comes out of the grass roots. Movements that stem from the "home office" of a church are rarely successful because they are conceived for the "in-general" promotion of religion; and although they may be successful, lasting growth usually comes from situations where "two or three are gathered together" in His name and where the Holy Spirit has moved the people to unite from a mutual sense of need.

It is interesting to realize that the group movement, in many instances, borders on an unorthodox approach. Although it deals with the ABC's of the Gospel, it often finds the minister unprepared for its new emphasis. Most alert clergymen, however, are eager to study any material available about the group movement. But it is hard to uncover, and so, if a leader is to find it, his experience must come, for the most part, from praying, working, and studying with those deeply involved—those who are sincere in their desire to deepen their faith, to help others in need, and to spread a practical application of the Gospel throughout the community. To my knowledge, there are no courses in the group movements in any theological seminary. Lectures on healing, personal witness, testimony, and prayer are rarely to be found. Yet the movement grows, and grows in different ways in the different churches. In the Episcopal Church it is generally along sane and traditional lines since most of the clergy and lay people prefer to operate in the climate of the Book of Common Prayer—through the anointing or the laying on of hands.

Generally speaking, there are great assets as well as dangers to be found in these group developments. On the positive side, we see remarkable evidences of the strengthening of faith, where a searching people find their needs fed through prayerful, healing associations in their own established churches. This is in contrast to a few years ago. Then, people were leaving their churches by the thousands in order to join the new and sincere religious movements that were springing up all over the land. Today, this process has ceased, and the group movement is now moving within the borders of the traditional churches. Today, with the blessing of the rectors, these churches are meeting the crises of those who have frustrating problems, illness, and personal tragedies. They are encouraging those who have a burning desire to share their deep personal experiences to meet with others.

181

In the Diocese of Pittsburgh, I can point to church after church where the priest has become a leader in this development and where, in great humility, he is meeting with his people, growing with them, and thus bringing new spiritual life and enthusiasm into the parish. Such groups are not necessarily large, and oftentimes they work for months and perhaps years without attracting more than a handful of participants. They are, however, the leaven for the future. They are bringing a new spirit into the parish as a whole and into the priest-in-charge in particular. One can point to thousands of transformed lives throughout America as a result of this growth.

On the negative side, we must take care that the healing movement does not become irrational and unscientific although, within the boundaries of my own diocese, I have seen almost no such evidence. Within prayer groups and evangelistic circles, the most obvious dangers are the possibility of self-righteousness on the part of those who work within the circle and a tendency toward antagonism on the part of those who are outside the circle. Warning must constantly be given to those within the groups of their responsibility to remain humble and, in many instances, silent. They must let their "light so shine" that others will want to seek their secret. Never should they give people the impression that unwise and loquacious zealots are bludgeoning them into another organization.

Witnessing and testifying to personal experience must be watched because it not only is magnetic but because it is capable of creating resistance to Christ. Oftentimes, the inner group becomes so self-righteous that they accuse anyone who resists their methods of being an advocate of the Devil. Our Lord reminds us frequently that He is the judge not we ourselves. If you want to build big muscles, you lift heavy weights and the resistance between the weights and muscles is the force that creates larger biceps. The one who desires to testify must beware lest he meet overt resistance in others, for he then becomes a weight and causes the would-be convert to build up a resisting energy which may cause him to move further from Christ during the rest of his life.

When we pick fruit, we know that it should be left on the tree and vine as long as it remains green. Pick green apples and eat them and there is going to be a disturbance of an unpleasant nature somewhere in the inward parts. To try to force, embarrass, buttonhole and bludgeon prospective converts is a sure way of driving them further from the Kingdom. We can offer bait, and if they show no interest, we must withdraw it. It is futile to try to catch fish by forced feeding.

When the group movement does not particularly appeal, those outside need not feel a sense of guilt because they have not seen fit to join. The minister must approach both the insiders and the outsiders with humility and Christian love. In so doing, he can save the movement from unwise zeal and self-righteousness. Likewise, he must save the outsiders from an unnecessary sense of guilt, exclusion, and general antagonism. To me, as I have said, it now seems conceivable that the hope of the future of Christianity may lie in this group movement. But we should realize that not everyone is ready for such an experience; and until that time comes, we must be most careful not to frighten those so far away that they can never find their way back.

Let us look at this matter of witness and personal testimony to religious experience and realize that there is more than one method of such expression. The people who publicly witness to what has happened to them are of great importance to the welfare of the Church, but their way is not the only method. It is important

184

that they do not consider themselves propagators of the only true way to Christian evangelism. When they feel that every Christian ought to make public statements and analyses of his inner experience, they are in danger of slipping into an unbearable kind of self-righteousness. Public testimony by word of mouth is of incalculable value, but sometimes the testifiers are liable to tell such personal tidbits about their lives that people are antagonized rather than helped by the stories. Such testimony can easily turn into egocentric, spiritual chitchat. This, too often, does not bring forth conversion. It brings revulsion instead.

Before people start giving testimony, there ought to be a prayerful study and a dutiful searching of one's conscience and intellect to determine both what should be said and what its effect will be upon others. Hit and miss impulsive testifying can degenerate into religious boredom and spiritual deflation. I have seen people become so intrigued with their own little stories about petty happenings in their lives that they have lost sight of the deep insights of the Gospel. They have so enjoyed speechmaking that they have brought themselves to the point where they have felt it discharges their entire obligation to others. They have blinded themselves to the need of becoming unheralded servants of Christ among the poor, the halt, the lame, and the blind. They have lost themselves in public utterance and have forgotten the importance of private service. Thus, we must be very careful about public testimony.

It seems to me that either a wise clergyman or a committee ought to censor, criticize, and evaluate the stories that are to be told and, after much prayer, decide when and where they are to be told. I speak with feeling because years ago I was, for a time, a zealot of the old Oxford group and was guilty of most of the mistakes, dangers and misconceptions that I have mentioned above. I still believe in testimony, but I am convinced that it must be handled and studied with care.

Temperamental differences in people should be given consideration. For example, it is relatively easy for me to talk about my spiritual experiences because I tend to be an extrovert. As a matter of fact, it is almost too easy for me to speak freely and feelingly about those things which have happened in my life and sometimes the ego creeps in, Christ is crowded out, and listeners are antagonized. On the other hand, my wife cannot express herself in this way. To her it would be a more than painful experience to glibly tell those inner secrets which she feels belong only to God and herself. She has a right to such a belief. She is better at doing good works than I am and more willing to serve in menial tasks for the benefit of the unfortunate than I can ever be. It would be unjust and self-righteous for me to judge her expression of Christianity as of less value than mine. Perhaps, the most powerful testimony in the long run is to be found in those who say nothing, but act with great poise and dedication through sacrificial deeds, generosity of possessions, and untiring services to insignificant (in the "world's" eyes) but needy people.

We must realize that some people are not able to work in groups and that associations of intimate personal relationships in religion are foreign to their training, experience, and background. These people should be dealt with in all kindness and understanding and be given other opportunities to serve Christ through the action of good work and sacrifice of time and ability. The minute we judge faithful communicants because they are not group-minded, we ourselves are guilty of disregarding the command of Our Lord, "Judge not, that ye be not judged."

It is important for us to remember that personal

187

testimony and witnessing to individual experience can be humble, winsome, and powerful. I have heard men of simple spiritual experience tell of the things that have happened to them through Christ and have seen their winsomeness draw others closer to our Lord. On the other hand, I have seen unskilled and unwise Christians who mistook the needs of their egos for witnessing to Christ turn those who listened away from God. To be well grounded in prayer and spiritual understanding is a prime requisite for the witnessing Christian.

A man came to me a few years ago who was deeply entrenched in alcohol and drugs. Through prayer, faith and work, God's Holy Spirit was able to change his life and free him from such captivity. He was fired with enthusiasm and said that he would like to announce his experience and conversion from the housetops. He wanted to know where he could start making speeches on the subject. I thought the matter over prayerfully, and then advised against it. Instead, I suggested that he pray to God that He would send people to him for assistance.

Several years later the former alcoholic came back and thanked me for my counsel. He said that for many

188

weeks after his healing, he had told no one about his experience. Finally, he said, when he was ready, his prayers were answered. Today, he can hardly fit into his life those addicts who want his help and call upon him for assistance. He is a great fisherman and rarely does he frighten away the catch but lures them with prayer and love and testimony until the subject desires deeply to be caught by Christ through His new and dedicated servant.

The Christian is called to be a fisherman. Now every wise fisherman knows that he must beware lest he scare the fish away. Fish must be approached quietly and with subtlety rather than with blatant noises and a lashing about in general.

The converts to new groups can well remember that St. Paul went away into the wilderness for three years after his conversion on the road to Damascus. He did not start burning up the Near East with evangelistic zeal until he had so digested his experience that he was ready to work with unceasing devotion and with great wisdom and caution.

It is well for us to remember that there is a spiritual tradition relating to secrecy in the Christian Church. In the earliest days of Christianity many symbols and signs were developed which were of a secret nature. This was not only to protect the Christians from physical violence but was also to protect the priceless Gospel from the error of "casting pearls before swine."

Just as the seed is nurtured in darkness and does not come to the light until the infant is developed and ready, so likewise should the Christian Gospel be nurtured amid small groups in secrecy until such time as God reveals that they are ready to tell others. To forget the wisdom of secrecy is to display unwisely our spiritual immaturity and thereby repel rather than magnetize those we would bring into the Holy Fellowship. The way of Christian caution is the right way to serve God in the long run. The call to evangelism—evangelism that carries with it love, wisdom, understanding, and tolerance—is our ever-present obligation. Having offered my cautions concerning it, may I add that to neglect the duty of evangelization would be a wrong judgment. Let us never forget that every Christian is called to be an evangelist in one way or another.

PAIN, SUFFERING, AND RIGHT JUDGMENT

CHAPTER SIXTEEN

PAIN, SUFFERING, AND
RIGHT JUDGMENT

To God, nothing is impossible. Yet, in spite of all our prayers, petitions, and searching, we are often burdened with some form of pain, suffering, or tragedy which must be carried throughout life on this earth. St. Paul himself symbolized a deep personal problem and handicap by referring to it as a "thorn in the flesh." "There was given to me," he says, "a thorn in the flesh, the messenger of Satan to buffet me, lest I should be exalted above measure." (*II Cor.* 12:7) Apparently, the thorn was with him to the end.

Why pain and suffering should be with mankind

193

is more than we can explain. We can only answer that they remain a mystery. Yet, this we do know: through them we can learn to think and see straight, and we can be led to victory and the opening of new vistas that cannot possibly be attained otherwise. A free translation of the mystifying phrase in the Lord's Prayer, "Lead us not into temptation," has been said to be, "Lead us successfully through difficulty to victory." And by the grace of God, that is exactly what can happen when the Christian is confronted with pain or a problem that is seemingly insurmountable.

Our diocese, as I have noted, has many healing groups and many prayer societies that are filled with people who are seeking a strength to carry on through the problems imposed by pain, environment, and circumstance. Many of these people are attractive and gifted, oftentimes to such a degree that they ordinarily might have little or nothing to do with the search for God and His truth if they were not forced to carry the burdens of their own pain or the responsibility for the pain of others. Instance after instance has proved that under the burden of a painful load many of these people have grown in knowledge and understanding and strength far beyond the mediocrity of their ordinary selves. Repeatedly, their almost insurmountable burdens have become their greatest blessings. More often than not, their crosses have not been lifted from their shoulders, but inward grace and courage has been infused to such a degree that they can carry them with dignity, grace, and joy.

Some have come to that place in life where they actually thank God for the suffering that has come to them; not in a spirit of resignation or acquiescence but rather in a cooperative attitude. They realize that He has done greater things for them through their suffering than they could ever have desired or deserved. They actually become thankful for their pain. Many Christians are now suffering gladly and will continue to suffer any amount of pain in return for the riches that God has revealed to them through it.

The object of Christianity is not to escape suffering but rather to meet it, since it is inescapable, and to come through it successfully. The wail of the Adam in us says, "What have I done to deserve this?" The voice of the follower of the Cross says, "What valuable lesson or experience will come to me through it? How will I be able to use it constructively?"

When we react to suffering with self-pity, we are

constructing a martyr complex which in turn does nothing but multiply our difficulties in exact ratio to the power we employ through our destructive thinking. To develop the habit of meeting our difficulties with self-pity is inexcusable. It creates a pitiable personality. On the other hand, to meet them with a stoical sense of endurance makes us hard, unsympathetic; and it offers no reward, achievement, or revelation. Buddha met suffering and taught his disciples to do likewise by denying all human desires. This tended to make people emotional blanks who cancelled their own God-given senses. Christianity takes suffering and turns it into a constructive power which leads us toward sure and certain victory.

On the other hand, the Mohammedan faces pain and suffering by saying that these are the will of God, and therefore there is nothing that anyone can do about them. Many misguided Christians think the way of the Moslem is the answer, but they are wrong. Jesus never denied the existence of evil or pain or suffering. He Himself suffered and told us that we also would suffer and that in our turn we would be compelled to carry our own crosses. But He also taught us not to despair at their weight—no matter how heavy. He promised us enough grace to lift any cross, whatsoever, and enough grace to do it with dignity and joy.

When in Korea on a preaching mission with the Air Force, I was invited to ride in the co-pilot's seat of a modern military transport. I was most impressed by the dozens of gadgets and meters and gauges above, in front of, beneath, and on either side of the pilot. The instruments indicated that there were resources within the aircraft to take care of almost any emergency faced by the pilot. This experience reminded me of the words of St. Paul when he told us that God had seen to it that we "come behind in no gift." Through him and His church, we all have the inner resources to meet any and every emergency.

One of the most important of the God-given inner resources is the gift of faith. By faith we do not mean a mere faith in one's self or in human nature or in a vague unknown future. By faith we do not mean a trust in those things of this earth which in the end will disappoint one. The hookup of faith must be made with God through Christ.

Let me tell you of a factual case that is in the process of unfoldment right now. A young couple I know have five children. Four are strapping and healthy.

197

One has been tragically handicapped and retarded. That one is Caroline. She walks a bit but can speak hardly a word. There is something wrong with a portion of her brain, and so her parents felt it best to put her in a special school for children who are handicapped. She was pathetically unhappy. Consequently, they removed her from the school in spite of the fact that many of the other children were happier there than they could be anywhere else. But for Caroline, it wasn't right. Due to the ordeal of separation she became desperately ill but still the doctors said that the only thing to do was to place her permanently in some institution and forget her as best they could.

But there was a loving mother in the picture with a simple greatness about her that can only be explained in one way—she is a living example of the Christian faith. Science said, with kindness, "forget Caroline"; but the mother had faith. She asked God for more and more strength and by regularly receiving the sacrament at Holy Communion and by constant praying, it was granted to her.

She developed a philosophy about Caroline. In brief, it was this. She said, "God gave Caroline to me this way and there is a reason for everything." She

198

did not blame herself or her husband or chastise herself for past sins, or confuse herself by asking why. She simply said, "Everything has a reason behind it, and God will open up a way for Caroline to serve Him and mankind." She further said, "I won't tell God how to heal her for if it is to be, it will be. All I want is God's purpose for Caroline and the rest of us to be fulfilled." The mother was almost the only one who fully believed. Fashionable friends and scientific minds said that she should face reality and not be stubborn. Everyone advised her to put the child away. The mother did face reality; not man's way, but God's way.

By a strange set of unforeseen and guided circumstances, an English woman came to live with them. She took charge of Caroline who was still a poor little wobbly thing whose brain was damaged and whose reflexes were impaired and whose whole life seemed to be that of a vacant body that feebly walked about without a mind. But Caroline did not seem that way to either the mother or to the English governess. They prayed constantly for God's purpose to be opened. One day, Caroline began to paint in strange and modernistic designs. Soon, from this child who appeared to be like an unoccupied house, there came fantastic lines and

199

colors and designs. Original lines and color combinations began to be put together in such an astonishing fashion that today at the age of twelve, she is regarded as an artistic genius. God has some wonder to express through her. She still has the impaired brain and speech and the vacant look, but when she starts to draw, it is as if there were a "mighty rushing wind" of strength working through her. Her lines are drawn with fantastic speed as though some great angel of art took over in her. I have seen it with my own eyes. I know what I am saying.

"Be of good cheer," said Jesus. "I have overcome the world."

THE PATIENCE TO STAND FIRM

CHAPTER SEVENTEEN

THE PATIENCE TO STAND FIRM

Faith is a gift of God rather than a quality of mind acquired by reason and intellect. It is necessary for all those who seek the will of God with dispassionate zeal to pray for continuing faith in the belief that victory lies ahead. If we believe that in the long run righteousness will always triumph, we can know the way of Christian accomplishment.

Most of us know what it means on occasions to have flashes of truth strike our conscious thoughts in moments of perplexity, and we know that at those times we are unwaveringly aware of what is right and what is

203

wrong. Yet, often the pressure of personal desire, public opinion, and the approval of our fellow men is stronger than our faith to stand by what we inwardly know to be right. Therefore, we compromise or become like Peter before the Crucifixion, denying that we ever knew Christ.

The agonies one causes himself through this wavering process loom in the memory like mountains of stupidity and fear. To be a member of a board or to be on an important civic committee and compromise by joining the wrong majority instead of the right minority is a most humbling experience. On the other hand, one can look back upon moments of strength whereby God gave the grace to take stands in the face of civil opposition and to know the joy of winning against odds. As a rule, it does not take long for a fickle majority to flop over to the right side.

A young Methodist preacher some years ago had just gone to a new church in southern Illinois, in the heart of the Ku Klux Klan territory. He was a fearless man and always stood for the right, no matter what the odds. He knew what the Klan was—domineering, arrogant, cruel, and intolerant, to put it mildly. When they came to him and arrogantly demanded that he have a

Sunday evening service for them, surprisingly enough, he granted their request. To prepare himself for that service, he went to Chicago to study the history and organization of the Klan and, of course, came back full of bitter thoughts. He knew exactly what he would have to say.

On the day of the great rally at which he was to be the preacher, the church was packed. The minister rose and told the assembled klansmen exactly what they stood for and what he thought about them. Then he told them what he believed in. He blazed away fearlessly for what was right, with the result that he was almost mobbed.

For days he had a bodyguard wherever he went and was loathed and despised throughout the community. The district superintendent of his church brought pressure to bear and tried to remove him, but he had a three-year contract and refused to budge. He was then offered a better cure in a more affluent community, but he stuck to his decision to sit out the storm of fury and hatred which whirled about him and his family.

That young minister rode out the storm. At the end of his three years, the whole temper of the town

205

had changed, and the Klan was discredited throughout the community. Earl Jewell, now an Episcopal clergyman in Kansas City, became a public hero—a result of the right judgment he had used to be patient and stand firm.

We must again warn of the danger of self-righteousness as we have repeatedly in this book. It is possible to take blind stands in the name of God and simply to be stubborn fools instead of wise, spiritual giants. As I write, I remember a man who has taken a self-righteous stand on a foolish issue. He has talked himself into the belief that his untruthful judgments are prompted by Christian sacrifice. Thus, he is spiritually blind because he is unwilling to look at the truth or believe that he can be wrong about anything. He is in holy orders and is highly educated in various intellectual pursuits, but he is probably one of the most tragically ignorant Christians I know.

How can Christianity show people of this type the meaning of truth? It probably cannot be done unless a man wants it. If he does not want objective reality, he does not want Christ, even though he may know all of the facts about Him, can pass all examinations about the Church and acquire all manner of degrees.

206

And there are many of us like this man. That is why we make such tragic mistakes in Christianity if we do not emphasize first things first when people seek training in the faith.

We never will and never can have a right judgment in anything if we base our premises on lies and self-deception or if we ease our consciences by knowledge of technicalities and rituals that pertain only to the periphery of the Christian religion. We can know all about Christ, and yet never *know* Him. And those of us in the former group are the modern scribes, hypocrites, and Pharisees against whom Jesus fights. We are the ones who now cause the Church such tragic tribulations.

All of us are bitten by this germ of evaluating second-things-first, to some degree, and it is the cause of the greatest battle of Christianity in every age. The battle reflects, however, the most basic of all sins—that of pride. Pride sets brains and judgments above the Spirit of Christ. Pride tricks us into believing that we are the most humble and faithful kind of Christian. Hideous forms of the anti-christ proceed to develop from this most destructive sin. The man of pride, in or outside the Church, unconsciously sets himself up as

207

God and from there on rationalizes or justifies his bad judgments.

Now, let us return to patience. It means that having arrived at a right judgment (through prayer, knowing the truth about ourselves, and the other processes that we have discussed in previous chapters), we must stand fast, knowing that Christ will bring sure and certain victory to us. We must ask for the grace to stand when at times it seems that every person has deserted us and that there is no earthly hope of winning the battle in which we are engaged.

Years ago, there was an event in intercollegiate swimming meets known as the "plunge." For some reason, it was eliminated in later years, but it was an interesting and exciting contest. As a rule, plungers were heavy men who stood at the end of the pool, dove deeply, and with outstretched hands floated as far as the momentum of their dive would carry them. The objective, as a rule, was to touch the end of the pool. When they were virtually out of breath and could barely stand it another second, the coach would kneel down and through cupped hands, cry, "Stick, stick." The plunger would strain and stretch and if he stuck just that extra second or two, invariably he touched the

208

end of the pool and was rewarded by reaching his objective and filling his lungs again with new fresh air.

When you are convinced that you have made a right decision and have acted upon it, stick it out and by the grace of God sure and certain victory will be accomplished.

"THE FOOL HATH SAID"

CHAPTER EIGHTEEN

"THE FOOL HATH SAID"

When the "fool hath said in his heart, there is no God," he has unconsciously set himself as his deity. Modern man does not often formally deny the existence of God but he has been so materially blessed that he lives under the misapprehension that his good fortunes are due solely to his own independent powers. Unconsciously, man sets himself up as his own deity because he forgets to realize that there is an original source of energy and life upon which he is totally dependent. If this power does not come from God, Himself, then man must be God. Surely, the power has to come from somewhere! The minute man's pride is so great that he unconsciously worships himself as his own god, he is on the way to sure and certain destruction. Sooner or later, he will face a crisis for which he has neither any answer nor any supply source of strength. What then?

Every man at some time in his life reaches a critical climax which is beyond the resources of his own or any other man's strength. This is a true description of the human or worldly situation, and it is the situation to which religion speaks. In fact, it is so true that we can agree wholeheartedly with the Communists when they taunt that religion is for the weak. That is just what it is. We accept the appraisal. But we are in violent disagreement with Soviet philosophy at a crucial point. In contrast to their conception of human nature, we affirm and state that every man—and this includes the hardened, communist man—is a fragile straw in the wind without the strengthening grace that comes from God. As Christians, realistic and not blinded by idealistic fancies, we cherish the truth that we are weak without a prayerful and sacramental relationship to God.

Let us ask the question, but to ask it is to answer it. Is any man strong when he reaches that crisis in

214

life which is more than he or any of his friends or any
human agency can handle? Human testimony throughout the ages shows that he is not. But instead of despair,
resentment, suicide or any one of the numerous human
ways of meeting the crisis, the Christian who realizes
this stalemating predicament should rejoice. Now the
supreme virtue of humility has a chance to creep into
his consciousness. If he stands alone and believes he is
strong enough for the crisis, nothing can be done but
to allow events to take their inevitable, crushing course.
With the humbling recognition that he is weak and can
not stand alone, there comes a new wisdom. A readi-
ness to perceive the deep meaning of the Christian
Gospel is now his good fortune. This has always been
his inheritance, but he has been too proud before to
claim it. Now he can accept it because he is ready.
Now he can truly rejoice.

When you sweep away all the fake façades of
people and get down to what they really are, when you
know their weaknesses, their lies, their fears, their hates,
and their pasts, will you find a strong man? Never!
Search as you may.

The person who does not have God to rely upon
must, as time goes on, find other props for support

Since anything less than God is passing, perishable, and unreliable, the materialistic prop-leaner is doomed to eventual decay. Again, let us ask a question. On what or on whom do you lean for support if you do not lean upon God? Do you lean on your family, your stocks, your business, your brains, your social standing, your physical attractiveness, your personal charm, your dominant power over people, or upon your physical strength? These, from one point of view, are good in their place. They are not intrinsically evil. But are they enough to lean upon? Are they permanent, stable, and free from destruction by accidents? How about one well-timed and well-placed H-bomb? Extreme as is the thought, one H-bomb can wipe out, not just one, but all of these in a few seconds. Then where are you, your prop, and your idol?

If you make props out of anything less than the power of God Himself, you are slipping into self-destruction. It is always, then, but a matter of time before you become absolutely helpless—whether you admit it or not. And this consequence of idol-worship, or prop-leaning, this inevitable consequence of our false judgment that places trust in something less than God is "bad news." Yet, such a consequence is the true and

216

desperate situation in which men find themselves when they put their faith in created things instead of in their Creator—the Father of Our Lord and Saviour, Jesus Christ.

If we have to rely only upon the props that our own egocentric judgment selects, we wind up in despair, frustration, or cynicism. And as long as we have faith only in props, there are no resources of the Christian religion that can help us. We are too proud for help; we choose to keep ourselves separated from God. We live by the "gospel of bad news."

For the humble man, the man who understands the profound nature of sin and its root connection with egocentric pride, there is another gospel. In contrast to the gospel of bad news, there is the Gospel of Christ. And as the word *gospel* literally means *good news,* the Gospel (or the Good News) of Christ is that you and I do not have to "go it alone" throughout life (unless we separate ourselves from God by pride). There is Someone who goes along with us, and by being with us shows us the meaning of love. To many people this seems to be no news at all, or at least unexciting.

The self-sufficient egoists are quite convinced from the start that they can very well make the journey under

217

their own steam, often without regard for their neighbor and often at his expense. Their success in the eyes of "the world" is often very marked. Of course, they do not take time to consider what happens after death—their range of vision is four score and ten—and they are quite blind to the degeneration that is happening to them right here in the middle of this life. That one can run out of steam and be rammed by the on-coming avalanche of events does not seem possible. The fact that one may need enough energy to propel one from this life to the next is rarely, if ever, given any consideration. The tragedy of the egoist lies in his naive notion that the power by which he lives and breathes is self-created and sustained.

Instead of one's power being self-created, the truth is quite otherwise. Whatever power man has, the egoist to the contrary, comes from the Creator and the Sustainer of life; and whatever redeeming power man receives in this world comes to him, if it comes at all, as the grace of God. The good news then is for those who are both humble and wise enough to know that every aspect of the life and the power they possess is given to them by a loving God. Alone and without God, man can only sink to despair, frustration, and cynicism.

218

"I am not ashamed of the gospel of Christ," says St. Paul: "for it is the power of God unto salvation to every one that believeth . . ." (*Rom.* 1:16). The Gospel, in other words, is the good news that the God who loves us and who can act in history has sent His power and strength to us in Christ. Christ came to redeem us, to save us from running amuck as we act and make choices and judgments with our self at the center of these actions, choices, and judgments. He came to save us from completely running down through lack of power or steam as we go on from moment to moment to please ourselves and unhappily thus learn, from bitter experience, that nothing really does.

Christ came, in other words, to save us from the malady which comes from the inflation of the ego whereby we believe that we are sufficient unto ourselves and can live life without the help of His grace and His love. This characteristic of self-sufficient man is what theologians mean by *sin*. It is willful separation of the creature from his Creator. But God "desireth not the death of a sinner." (*P.B.*, p. 7.) His Universe operates by love, and although our separating pride is offensive, God has the mysterious power of forgiveness which has been bestowed on us through the life and

219

death of our Lord Jesus Christ. As the Declaration of Absolution says: "He pardoneth and absolveth all those who truly repent, and unfeignedly believe his holy Gospel." (*P.B.*, p. 7.) Forgiveness, thus, is the power which God bestows upon us when we come to the knowledge that we must set aside our egos as supreme and acknowledge Him as King. Is it better expressed than in the words of a hymn by H. W. Baker?

> The King of love my shepherd is,
> Whose goodness faileth never;
> I nothing lack if I am his.
> And he is mine for ever. (*Hymn* 345)

God has a plan for us. It is not an inflexible blueprint but an overall picture which we are called to gaze upon and to imitate. He made us in His own image and showed us what that image is like by sending us His son, Jesus Christ. Two aspects of the plan stand out. First, self-centered and "fallen" man needs to see what a redeemed man is like in action. Thus, the Incarnation is the part of God's overall plan that shows God's image in action. Second, God, who is the Sustainer as well as the Creator, provides the means to help the humble and penitent man in his fight to overcome pride and separation from the source and meaning of life. Thus, Christ established as part of God's plan a Church, and this gave us a Bible, a redemptive fellowship, and a sacramental system as channels for bringing to us the grace for our true task.

Left to our own devices, and allowed to falsely believe that we have to "go it alone," we make wrong judgments and these taint all things that we touch. Renouncing our own devices and choosing to live a Christian life of prayer and communion, we are on the way to "a right judgment in all things." May we not look once more at Our Ancient Guide, and pray with all the humble Christians of our day and of the ages past the Collect for Whitsunday?

O God, who as at this time didst teach the hearts of thy faithful people, by sending to them the light of thy Holy Spirit; Grant us by the same Spirit to have a right judgment in all things, and evermore to rejoice in his holy comfort; through the merits of Christ Jesus our Saviour, who liveth and reigneth with thee, in the unity of the same Spirit, one God, world without end. *Amen.*

EPILOGUE

EPILOGUE

Matthew 14:25-33

"And in the fourth watch of the night Jesus went unto them, walking on the sea. And when the disciples saw him walking on the sea, they were troubled, saying, It is a spirit; and they cried out for fear. But straightway, Jesus spake unto them, saying, Be of good cheer; it is I; be not afraid. And Peter answered him and said, Lord, if it be thou, bid me come unto thee on the water. And he said, Come. And when Peter was come down out of the ship, he walked on the water, to go to Jesus. But when he saw the wind boisterous, he was afraid; and beginning to sink, he cried, saying, Lord, save me. And immediately Jesus stretched forth his hand, and caught him, and said unto him. O thou of little faith, wherefore didst thou doubt? And when they were come into the ship, the wind ceased. Then they that were in the ship

225

came and worshipped him, saying, Of a truth thou art the Son of God."

At the fourth watch, or about three o'clock in the morning, our Lord's mind was clear, His future definite, His decisions made. All uncertainty had left His consciousness. He rose from His place of communion with His Father and started down the familiar mountainside. In the darkness below, He could look far out upon the Sea of Galilee as it was intermittently illumined by the great flashes of lightning.

Halfway across the sea, the disciples were desperately trying to keep their boat from capsizing as they were buffeted by the wind and the waves. They were frightened by the streaks of fire that flashed out of the heavens. Suddenly, Peter looked up and saw a luminous figure approaching. It seemed to be walking upon the water. At first, when he called attention to it, the disciples thought it was a ghost. But Peter, the perceptive, began to be aware of the fact that it might be Jesus.

At this point, some of us may stop and say that we prefer not to be asked to believe the story of Jesus walking on the water. Yet, why should we disbelieve it? I feel about it something like this: If my beautiful white

226

nylon vestments can be made from coal, if mere human beings can make rubber out of alcohol, if insignificant man can fly faster than the speed of sound, if man can project pictures and voices over hundreds of miles to be produced in a living room on a screen without the assistance of wires or cables and do a thousand and one other modern miracles, does it seem impossible for the Son of Man to have walked upon the water of the Sea of Galilee, if He chose so to do?

Peter cupped his hands about his mouth and cried out a question over the waves. Was the apparition Jesus? The Master quickly answered in the affirmative. Then, Peter cried out that if it was indeed our Lord, He should bid him walk to Him on the water. Jesus quickly answered, "Come."

Now you can see Peter the bold, not even stopping to think, but climbing out of the boat and, to the utter astonishment of everyone, starting to walk upon the water with unwavering steps and with powerful strides. Suddenly, as the spray of the great waves hit him, *doubt* arose. He said to himself, "Peter, what in heaven's name are you doing out here? Are you crazy? Do you think you are walking upon the water? What would happen if you should sink in this storm?"

227

He sank immediately. Sputtering, he pawed the air, fighting to keep afloat. "Lord, save me," he cried.

Jesus reached out His hand and lifted Peter with effortless touch and helped him back into the boat. Then, looking at him with tender disappointment, He said: "Oh, Peter, why did you doubt?"

The sea became calm and the frightened, drenched disciples hovered at the feet of Jesus saying, "Truly you are the Son of God."

The disciples had said this before, but they constantly needed the presence of Jesus to remind them physically of the great truths of God made possible through faith in Him as the Revelation. When Christ is recognized as the Saviour the frustrating storms of life can be calmed and judgments that might otherwise stem from fear and despair can then stem from the peace of God that passeth all understanding. And can judgments that are right come from a rough, stormy, fearful inner life? Or should we remember in the words of the psalmist:

God is our refuge and strength, a very present help in trouble. Therefore will not we fear, though the earth be removed, and though the mountains be carried into the midst of the sea; Though the waters thereof roar and be troubled, though the mountains shake with the swelling thereof. . . . Be still, and know that I am God. (*Ps.* 46.)

Those of us who seek to make decisions with God the Father, in the name of God the Son, through the guidance of God the Holy Spirit, will be able to walk on top of, beneath, or even through, the boiling waters of our times, for by the help of the blessed Trinity, we can obtain "a right judgment in all things" and be provided with the means of grace by which we may perform the same.

INDEX

INDEX

90-254-HC-13